This edition published by Spark Publishing

Spark Publishing
A Division of SparkNotes LLC
120 Fifth Avenue, 8th Floor
New York, NY 10011

Please submit all comments and questions or report errors to www.sparknotes.com/errors

Printed and bound in the United States

ISBN 1-58663-414-3

Introduction:
Stopping to Buy SparkNotes on a Snowy Evening

Whose words these are you *think* you know.
Your paper's due tomorrow, though;
We're glad to see you stopping here
To get some help before you go.

Lost your course? You'll find it here.
Face tests and essays without fear.
Between the words, good grades at stake:
Get great results throughout the year.

Once school bells caused your heart to quake
As teachers circled each mistake.
Use SparkNotes and no longer weep,
Ace every single test you take.

Yes, books are lovely, dark, and deep,
But only what you grasp you keep,
With hours to go before you sleep,
With hours to go before you sleep.

CONTENTS

CONTEXT

ORA NEALE HURSTON WAS BORN on January 7, 1891, in Notasulga, Alabama, to John Hurston, a carpenter and Baptist preacher, and Lucy Potts Hurston, a former schoolteacher. Hurston was the fifth of eight children, and while she was still a toddler, her family moved to Eatonville, Florida, the first all-black incorporated town in the United States, where John Hurston served several terms as mayor. In 1917, Hurston enrolled in Morgan Academy in Baltimore, where she completed her high school education.

Three years later, she enrolled at Howard University and began her writing career. She took classes there intermittently for several years and eventually earned an associate degree. The university's literary magazine published her first story in 1921. In 1925, she moved to New York and became a significant figure in the Harlem Renaissance. A year later, she, Langston Hughes, and Wallace Thurman organized the journal *Fire!*, considered one of the defining publications of the era. Meanwhile, she enrolled in Barnard College and studied anthropology with arguably the greatest anthropologist of the twentieth century, Franz Boas. Hurston's life in Eatonville and her extensive anthropological research on rural black folklore greatly influenced her writing.

Their Eyes Were Watching God was published in 1937, long after the heyday of the Harlem Renaissance. The literature of the 1920s, a period of postwar prosperity, was marked by a sense of freedom and experimentation, but the 1930s brought the Depression and an end to the cultural openness that had allowed the Harlem Renaissance to flourish. As the Depression worsened, political tension increased within the United States; cultural production came to be dominated by "social realism," a gritty, political style associated with left-wing radicalism. The movement's proponents felt that art should be primarily political and expose social injustice in the world. This new crop of writers and artists dismissed much of the Harlem Renaissance as bourgeois, devoid of important political content and thus devoid of any artistic merit. The influential and highly political black novelist Richard Wright, then an ardent Communist, wrote a scathing review of *Their Eyes Were Watching God* upon its publication, claiming that it was not "serious fiction" and that it "carries no theme, no message, no thought."

Hurston was also criticized for her comportment: she refused to bow to gender conventions, and her behavior often seemed shocking if not outrageous. Although she won a Guggenheim Fellowship and had published prolifically (both works of fiction and anthropological works), Hurston fell into obscurity for a number of years. By the late 1940s, she began to have increasing difficulty getting her work published. By the early 1950s, she was forced to work as a maid. In the 1960s, the counterculture revolution continued to show disdain for any literature that was not overtly political, and Zora Neale Hurston's writing was further ignored.

A stroke in the late 1950s forced Hurston to enter a welfare home in Florida. After she died penniless on January 28, 1960, she was buried in an unmarked grave. Alice Walker, another prominent African-American writer, rediscovered her work in the late 1960s. In 1973, Walker traveled to Florida to place a marker on Hurston's grave containing the phrase: "A Genius of the South." Walker's 1975 essay "In Search of Zora Neale Hurston," published in *Ms.* magazine, propelled Hurston's work back into vogue. Since then, Hurston's opus has been published and republished many times; it has even been adapted for the cinema: Spike Lee's first feature film, *She's Gotta Have It,* parallels *Their Eyes Were Watching God* and can be viewed as an interesting modern adaptation of the novel.

One of the strengths of Hurston's work is that it can be studied in the context of a number of different American literary traditions. Most often, *Their Eyes Were Watching God* is associated with Harlem Renaissance literature, even though it was published in a later era, because of Hurston's connection to that scene. Certain aspects of the book, though, make it possible to discuss it in other literary contexts. For example, some critics argue that the novel should be read in the context of American Southern literature: with its rural Southern setting and its focus on the relationship between man and nature, the dynamics of human relationships, and a hero's quest for independence, *Their Eyes Were Watching God* fits well into the tradition that includes such works as Mark Twain's *The Adventures of Huckleberry Finn* and William Faulkner's *The Sound and the Fury.* The novel is also important in the continuum of American feminist literature, comparing well to Kate Chopin's *The Awakening.* More specifically, and due in large part to Alice Walker's essay, Zora Neale Hurston is often viewed as the first in a succession of great American black women writers that includes Alice Walker, Toni Morrison, and Gloria Naylor. But *Their Eyes Were Watching God* resists reduction to a single movement, either literary or political. Wright's criticism from 1937 is, to a certain extent, true: the book is not a political treatise—it carries no single, overwhelming message or moral. Far from being a weakness, however, this resistance is the secret of the novel's strength: it is a profoundly rich, multifaceted work that can be read in a number of ways.

PLOT OVERVIEW

J ANIE CRAWFORD, an attractive, confident, middle-aged black woman, returns to Eatonville, Florida, after a long absence. The black townspeople gossip about her and speculate about where she has been and what has happened to her young husband, Tea Cake. They take her confidence as aloofness, but Janie's friend Pheoby Watson sticks up for her. Pheoby visits her to find out what has happened. Their conversation frames the story that Janie relates.

Janie explains that her grandmother raised her after her mother ran off. Nanny loves her granddaughter and is dedicated to her, but her life as a slave and experience with her own daughter, Janie's mother, has warped her worldview. Her primary desire is to marry Janie as soon as possible to a husband who can provide security and social status for her. She finds a much older farmer named Logan Killicks and insists that Janie marry him.

After moving in with Logan, Janie is miserable. Logan is pragmatic and unromantic and, in general, treats her like a pack mule. One day, Joe Starks, a smooth-tongued and ambitious man, ambles down the road in front of the farm. He and Janie flirt in secret for a couple weeks before she runs off and marries him.

Janie and Jody, as she calls him, travel to all-black Eatonville, where Jody hopes to have a "big voice." A consummate politician, Jody soon succeeds in becoming the mayor, postmaster, storekeeper, and the biggest landlord in town. But Janie seeks something more than a man with a big voice. She soon becomes disenchanted with the monotonous, stifling life that she shares with Jody. She wishes that she could be a part of the rich social life in town, but Jody doesn't allow her to interact with "common" people. Jody sees Janie as the fitting ornament to his wealth and power, and he tries to shape her into his vision of what a mayor's wife should be. On the surface, Janie silently submits to Jody; inside, however, she remains passionate and full of dreams.

After almost two decades of marriage, Janie finally asserts herself. When Jody insults her appearance, Janie rips him to shreds in front of the townspeople, telling them all how ugly and impotent he is. In retaliation, he savagely beats her. Their marriage breaks down, and Jody becomes quite ill. After months without interacting, Janie goes in to visit him on his deathbed. Refusing to be silenced, she once again chastises him for the way that he treated her. As she berates him, he dies.

After Jody's funeral, Janie feels free for the first time in years. She rebuffs various suitors who come to court her because she loves her newfound independence. But when Tea Cake, a man twelve years her junior, enters her life, Janie immediately senses a spark of mutual attraction. She begins dating Tea Cake despite critical gossip within the town. To everyone's shock, Janie then marries Tea Cake nine months after Jody's death, sells Jody's store, and leaves town to go with Tea Cake to Jacksonville.

During the first week of their marriage, Tea Cake and Janie encounter difficulties. He steals her money and leaves her alone one night, making her think that he married her only for her money. But he returns, explaining that he never meant to leave her and that his theft occurred in a moment of weakness. Afterward, they promise to share all their experiences and opinions with each other. They move to the Everglades, where they work during the harvest season and socialize during the summer off-season. Tea Cake's quick wit and friendliness make their shack the center of entertainment and social life.

A terrible hurricane bursts into the Everglades two years after Janie and Tea Cake's marriage. As they desperately flee the rising waters, a rabid dog bites Tea Cake. At the time, Tea Cake doesn't realize the dog's condition; three weeks later, however, he falls ill. During a rabies-induced bout of madness, Tea Cake becomes convinced that Janie is cheating on him. He starts firing a pistol at her and Janie is forced to kill him to save her life. She is immediately put on trial for murder, but the all-white, all-male jury finds her not guilty. She returns to Eatonville where her former neighbors are ready to spin malicious gossip about her circumstances, assuming that Tea Cake has left her and taken her money. Janie wraps up her recounting to Pheoby, who is greatly impressed by Janie's experiences. Back in her room that night, Janie feels at one with Tea Cake and at peace with herself.

CHARACTER LIST

Janie Mae Crawford The protagonist of the novel. Janie defies
categorization: she is black but flaunts her Caucasian-
like straight hair, which comes from her mixed
ancestry; she is a woman but defies gender stereotypes
by insisting on her independence and wearing overalls.
Behind her defiance are a curiosity and confidence that
drive her to experience the world and become
conscious of her relation to it. Part of Janie's
maturity rests in her ability to realize that others'
cruelty toward her or their inability to understand her
stems not from malice but from their upbringing or
limited perspective.

Tea Cake   Janie's third husband and first real love. Twelve years
younger than Janie, Tea Cake impresses her with his
quick wit and zest for living. But behind the flash, he
has a real affection for, and understanding of, Janie. He
doesn't try to force Janie to be anything other than
herself, and he treats her with respect. He is not
without faults, however; he does steal from her once
and beat her. These reprehensible incidents, though,
make him a more real character than one who
possesses only idealized positive qualities.

Jody Starks Janie's second husband. Jody, as Janie calls him, travels
from Georgia to Eatonville to satisfy his ambition and
hunger for power. A consummate politician and
businessman, he becomes the postmaster, mayor,
storekeeper, and biggest landlord in Eatonville. But he
treats Janie as an object rather than a person, and their
marriage deteriorates.

Logan Killicks Janie's first husband. Nanny arranges Janie's marriage to Logan because she values financial security and respectability over love. Logan pampers Janie for a year before he tries to make her help him with the farming work. Feeling used and unloved, Janie leaves him for Jody Starks.

Pheoby Watson Janie's best friend in Eatonville. Pheoby gives Janie the benefit of the doubt when the townspeople gossip viciously about Janie. She is the audience for Janie's story and her presence is occasionally felt in the colloquial speech that the narrator mixes in with a more sophisticated narrative style.

Nanny Crawford Janie's grandmother. Nanny's experience as a slave stamped her worldview with a strong concern for financial security, respectability, and upward mobility. These values clash with Janie's independence and desire to experience the world, though Janie comes to respect Nanny's values and decisions as well intended.

Mr. and Mrs. Turner Everglades residents who run a small restaurant. Mrs. Turner prides herself on her Caucasian features and disdains anyone with a more African appearance. She worships Janie because of her Caucasian features. She cannot understand why a woman like Janie would marry a man as dark as Tea Cake, and she wants to introduce Janie to her brother.

Sam Watson Pheoby's husband. Sam Watson is a source of great humor and wisdom during the conversations on Jody's porch. When a few Eatonville residents begin to express their resentment toward Jody, Sam acknowledges that Jody can be overbearing and commanding but points out that Jody is responsible for many improvements in the town.

Leafy Crawford Janie's mother. Leafy was born shortly before the end of the Civil War and ran away after giving birth to Janie.

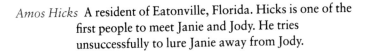

Amos Hicks A resident of Eatonville, Florida. Hicks is one of the first people to meet Janie and Jody. He tries unsuccessfully to lure Janie away from Jody.

Motor Boat One of Tea Cake and Janie's friends in the Everglades. Motor Boat flees the hurricane with them and weathers the storm in an abandoned house.

Hezekiah Potts The delivery boy and assistant shopkeeper at Jody's store. After Jody's death, Hezekiah begins to mimic Jody's affectations.

Dr. Simmons A friendly white doctor who is well known in the muck.

Johnny Taylor A young man whom Janie kisses when she starts to feel sexual desires at age sixteen. This incident prompts Nanny to force Janie to marry the more socially respectable Logan Killicks.

Annie Tyler and Who Flung A wealthy widow who lived in Eatonville, and her much younger fiancé, who took her money and fled at the first opportunity. Early in her marriage to Tea Cake, Janie fears that he will turn out to be like Who Flung and that she will end up like Annie Tyler.

Mr. and Mrs. Washburn Nanny's employers after she became a free woman. Nanny lived in a house in the Washburn's backyard, and they helped raise Janie with their own children.

Nunkie A girl in the Everglades who flirts relentlessly with Tea Cake. Janie grows extremely jealous of Nunkie, but after Tea Cake reassures her that Nunkie means nothing to him, Nunkie disappears from the novel.

ANALYSIS OF MAJOR CHARACTERS

JANIE

Although *Their Eyes Were Watching God* revolves around Janie's relationships with other people, it is first and foremost a story of Janie's search for spiritual enlightenment and a strong sense of her own identity. When we first and last see Janie, she is alone. The novel is not the story of her quest for a partner but rather that of her quest for a secure sense of independence. Janie's development along the way can be charted by studying her use of language and her relationship to her own voice.

At the end of her journey, Janie returns to Eatonville a strong and proud woman, but at the beginning of her story, she is unsure of who she is or how she wants to live. When she tells her story to Pheoby, she begins with her revelation under the blossoming pear tree—the revelation that initiates her quest. Under the pear tree, she witnesses a perfect union of harmony within nature. She knows that she wants to achieve this type of love, a reciprocity that produces oneness with the world, but is unsure how to proceed. At this point, she is unable to articulate even to herself exactly what she wants.

When Jody Starks enters her life, he seems to offer the ideal alternative to the dull and pragmatic Logan Killicks. With his ambitious talk, Jody convinces Janie that he will use his thirst for conquest to help her realize her dreams, whatever they may be. Janie learns that Jody's exertion of power only stifles her. But just before Jody's death, Janie's repressed power breaks through in a torrent of verbal retaliation. Her somewhat cruel tirade at the dying Jody measures the depth of Jody's suppression of her inner life. Having begun to find her voice, Janie blows through social niceties to express herself.

Janie flourishes in her relationship with Tea Cake, as he "teaches her the maiden language all over." Her control of speech reaches a new level as she learns to be silent when she chooses. This idea of silence as strength rather than passivity comes to the forefront during Janie's trial, when the narrator glosses over her testimony. Dialogue has been pivotally important up to this point, and one might expect Hurston to use the courtroom scene to showcase Janie's hard-won, mature voice. The absence of dialogue here, Mary Ellen Washington argues in the foreword present in most editions of the novel, reflects Hurston's discomfort with rhetoric for its own sake; Hurston doesn't want Janie's voice to be confused with that of the lawyer or politician. Janie's development of her voice is inseparable from her inner growth, and the drama of the courtroom may be too contrived to draw out the nuances of her inner life. Janie summarizes the novel's attitude toward language when she tells Pheoby that talking "don't amount tuh uh hill uh beans" if it isn't connected to actual experience.

TEA CAKE

Tea Cake functions as the catalyst that helps drive Janie toward her goals. Like all of the other men in Janie's life, he plays only a supporting role. Before his arrival, Janie has already begun to find her own voice, as is demonstrated when she finally stands up to Jody. As we see at the end of the novel, after Tea Cake's death, Janie remains strong and hopeful; therefore, it's fair to say that Janie is not dependent on Tea Cake. Nevertheless, he does play a crucial role in her development.

When she meets Tea Cake, Janie has already begun to develop a strong, proud sense of self, but Tea Cake accelerates this spiritual growth. Ever since her moment under the pear tree, Janie has known that she will find what she is searching for only through love. In Tea Cake she finds a creative and vivacious personality who enjoys probing the world around him and respects Janie's need to develop. Whereas Logan treats her like a farm animal and Jody silences her, Tea Cake converses and plays with her. Instead of stifling her personality, he encourages it, introducing her to new experiences and skills.

While Tea Cake is vital to Janie's development, he is not an indispensable part of her life, a crucial truth that is revealed when Janie shoots him. He plays a role in her life, helping her to better understand herself. By teaching her how to shoot a gun, ironically, he provides her with the tools that ultimately kill him. Janie's decision to save herself rather than yield her life up to the crazy Tea Cake points to her increasing sense of self and demonstrates that Tea Cake's ultimate function in the novel is not to make Janie dependent on him for happiness but to help her find happiness and security within herself.

JODY STARKS

Jody's character is opposite that of Tea Cake. He is cruel, conceited, and uninterested in Janie as a person. But his cruelty is not a result of any specific animosity toward Janie; rather, it is a reflection of the values that he holds and the way that he understands his relationship to the world. Jody depends on the exertion of power for his sense of himself; he is only happy and secure when he feels that he holds power over those around him. In Janie's words, he needs to "have [his] way all [his] life, trample and mash down and then die ruther than tuh let [him]self heah 'bout it." He needs to feel like a "big voice," a force of "irresistible maleness" before whom the whole world bows.

In order to maintain this illusion of irresistible power, Jody tries to dominate everyone and everything around him. His entire existence is based on purchasing, building, bullying, and political planning. He marries Janie not because he loves her as a person but because he views her as an object that will serve a useful purpose in his schemes. She is young, beautiful, and stately, and thus fits his ideal of what a mayor's wife should be. Jody is obsessed with notions of power, and Janie remains unfulfilled by their relationship because these notions require her to be a mute, static object and prevent her from growing. He forces her to tie her hair up because its phallic quality threatens his male dominance and because its feminine beauty makes him worry that he will lose her. Janie ultimately rebels against Jody's suppression of her, and by toppling his secure sense of his own power, she destroys his will to live.

THEMES, MOTIFS & SYMBOLS

THEMES

Themes are the fundamental and often universal ideas explored in a literary work.

LANGUAGE: SPEECH AND SILENCE

Their Eyes Were Watching God is most often celebrated for Hurston's unique use of language, particularly her mastery of rural Southern black dialect. Throughout the novel, she utilizes an interesting narrative structure, splitting the presentation of the story between high literary narration and idiomatic discourse. The long passages of discourse celebrate the culturally rich voices of Janie's world; these characters speak as do few others in American literature, and their distinctive grammar, vocabulary, and tone mark their individuality.

Hurston's use of language parallels Janie's quest to find her voice. As Henry Louis Gates Jr. writes in the afterword to most modern editions of the book, *Their Eyes Were Watching God* is primarily concerned "with the project of finding a voice, with language as an instrument of injury and salvation, of selfhood and empowerment." Jody stifles Janie's speech, as when he prevents her from talking after he is named mayor; her hatred of him stems from this suppression of her individuality. Tea Cake, on the other hand, engages her speech, conversing with her and putting himself on equal terms with her; her love for him stems from his respect for her individuality.

After Janie discovers her ability to define herself by her speech interactions with others, she learns that silence too can be a source of empowerment; having found her voice, she learns to control it. Similarly, the narrator is silent in conspicuous places, neither revealing why Janie isn't upset with Tea Cake's beating nor disclosing her words at the trial. In terms of both the form of the novel and its thematic content, Hurston places great emphasis on the control of language as the source of identity and empowerment.

POWER AND CONQUEST AS MEANS TO FULFILLMENT

Whereas Janie struggles to assert a place for herself by undertaking a spiritual journey toward love and self-awareness, Jody attempts to achieve fulfillment through the exertion of power. He tries to purchase and control everyone and everything around him; he exercises his authority hoping to subordinate his environment to his will. He labors under the illusion that he can control the world around him and that, by doing so, he will achieve some sense of profound fulfillment. Others exhibit a similar attitude toward power and control; even Tea Cake, for example, is filled with hubris as the hurricane whips up, certain that he can survive the storm through his mastery of the muck. For both Jody and Tea Cake, the natural world reveals the limits of human power. In Jody's case, as disease sets in, he begins to lose the illusion that he can control his world; the loss of authority over Janie as she talks back to him furthers this disillusionment. In Tea Cake's case, he is forced to flee the hurricane and struggles to survive the ensuing floods. This limit to the scope of one's power proves the central problem with Jody's power-oriented approach toward achieving fulfillment: ultimately, Jody can neither stop his deterioration nor silence Janie's strong will.

LOVE AND RELATIONSHIPS VERSUS INDEPENDENCE

Their Eyes Were Watching God is the story of how Janie achieves a strong sense of self and comes to appreciate her independence. But her journey toward enlightenment is not undertaken alone. The gender differences that Hurston espouses require that men and women provide each other things that they need but do not possess. Janie views fulfilling relationships as reciprocal and based on mutual respect, as demonstrated in her relationship with Tea Cake, which elevates Janie into an equality noticeably absent from her marriages to Logan and Jody.

Although relationships are implied to be necessary to a fulfilling life, Janie's quest for spiritual fulfillment is fundamentally a self-centered one. She is alone at the end yet seems content. She liberates herself from her unpleasant and unfulfilling relationships with Logan and Jody, who hinder her personal journey. Through her relationship with Tea Cake, Janie experiences true fulfillment and enlightenment and becomes secure in her independence. She feels a deep connection to the world around her and even feels that the spirit of Tea Cake is with her. Thus, even though she is alone, she doesn't feel alone.

MOTIFS

Motifs are recurring structures, contrasts, or literary devices that can help to develop and inform the text's major themes.

COMMUNITY

As Janie returns to Eatonville, the novel focuses on the porch-sitters who gossip and speculate about her situation. In Eatonville and the Everglades, particularly, the two most significant settings in the novel, Janie constantly interacts with the community around her. At certain times, she longs to be a part of this vibrant social life, which, at its best, offers warmth, safety, connection, and interaction for Janie. In Chapter 18, for example, when Tea Cake, Janie, and Motor Boat seek shelter from the storm, the narrator notes that they "sat in company with the others in other shanties"; of course, they are not literally sitting in the same room as these others, but all of those affected by the hurricane share a communal bond, united against the overwhelming, impersonal force of the hurricane.

At other times, however, Janie scorns the pettiness of the gossip and rumors that flourish in these communities, which often criticize her out of jealousy for her independence and strong will. These communities, exemplifying a negative aspect of unity, demand the sacrifice of individuality. Janie refuses to make this sacrifice, but even near the end of the book, during the court trial, "it [i]s not death she fear[s]. It [i]s misunderstanding." In other words, Janie still cares what people in the community think because she still longs to understand herself.

RACE AND RACISM

Because Zora Neale Hurston was a famous black author who was associated with the Harlem Renaissance, many readers assume that *Their Eyes Were Watching God* is concerned primarily with issues of race. Although race is a significant motif in the book, it is not, by any means, a central theme. As Alice Walker writes in her dedication to *I Love Myself When I Am Laughing . . . and Then Again When I Am Looking Mean and Impressive: A Zora Neale Hurston Reader,* "I think we are better off if we think of Zora Neale Hurston as an artist, period—rather than as the artist/politician most black writers have been required to be." Along the same lines, it is far more fulfilling to read Janie's story as a profoundly human quest than as a distinctly black one.

But issues of race are nonetheless present. Janie and Tea Cake experience prejudice from both blacks and whites at significant moments in the book. Two moments in particular stand out: Janie's interactions, in Chapter 16, with Mrs. Turner, a black woman with racist views *against blacks,* and the courtroom scene, in Chapter 19, after which Janie is comforted by white women but scorned by her black friends. In these moments, we see that racism in the novel operates as a cultural construct, a free-floating force that affects anyone, white or black, weak enough to succumb to it. Hurston's perspective on racism was undoubtedly influenced by her study with influential anthropologist Franz Boas, who argued that ideas of race are culturally constructed and that skin color indicates little, if anything, about innate difference. In other words, racism is a cultural force that individuals can either struggle against or yield to rather than a mindset rooted in demonstrable facts. In this way, racism operates in the novel just like the hurricane and the doctrine to which Jody adheres; it is an environmental force that challenges Janie in her quest to achieve harmony with the world around her.

THE FOLKLORE QUALITY OF RELIGION

As the title indicates, God plays a huge role in the novel, but this God is not really the Judeo-Christian god. The book maintains an almost Gnostic perspective on the universe: God is not a single entity but a diffuse force. This outlook is particularly evident in the mystical way that Hurston describes nature. At various times, the sun, moon, sky, sea, horizon, and other aspects of the natural world appear imbued with divinity. The God in the title refers to these divine forces throughout the world, both beautiful and threatening, that Janie encounters. Her quest is a spiritual one because her ultimate goal is to find her place in the world, understand who she is, and be at peace with her environment.

Thus, except for one brief reference to church in Chapter 12, organized religion never appears in the novel. The idea of spirituality, on the other hand, is always present, as the novel espouses a worldview rooted in folklore and mythology. As an anthropologist, Hurston collected rural mythology and folklore of blacks in America and the Caribbean. Many visions of mysticism that she presents in the novel—her haunting personification of Death, the idea of a sun-god, the horizon as a boundary at the end of the world—are likely culled directly from these sources. Like her use of dialogue, Hurston's presentation of folklore and non-Christian spirituality celebrates the black rural culture.

Symbols

Symbols are objects, characters, figures, or colors used to represent abstract ideas or concepts.

Hair

Janie's hair is a symbol of her power and unconventional identity; it represents her strength and individuality in three ways. First, it represents her independence and defiance of petty community standards. The town's critique at the very beginning of the novel demonstrates that it is considered undignified for a woman of Janie's age to wear her hair down. Her refusal to bow down to their norms clearly reflects her strong, rebellious spirit. Second, her hair functions as a phallic symbol; her braid is constantly described in phallic terms and functions as a symbol of a typically masculine power and potency, which blurs gender lines and thus threatens Jody. Third, her hair, because of its straightness, functions as a symbol of whiteness; Mrs. Turner worships Janie because of her straight hair and other Caucasian characteristics. Her hair contributes to the normally white male power that she wields, which helps her disrupt traditional power relationships (male over female, white over black) throughout the novel.

The Pear Tree and the Horizon

The pear tree and the horizon represent Janie's idealized views of nature. In the bees' interaction with the pear tree flowers, Janie witnesses a perfect moment in nature, full of erotic energy, passionate interaction, and blissful harmony. She chases after this ideal throughout the rest of the book. Similarly, the horizon represents the far-off mystery of the natural world, with which she longs to connect. Janie's hauling in of her horizon "like a great fish-net" at the end of the novel indicates that she has achieved the harmony with nature that she has sought since the moment under the pear tree.

The Hurricane

The hurricane represents the destructive fury of nature. As such, it functions as the opposite of the pear tree and horizon imagery: whereas the pear tree and horizon stand for beauty and pleasure, the hurricane demonstrates how chaotic and capricious the world can be. The hurricane makes the characters question who they are and what their place in the universe is. Its impersonal nature—it is simply a force of pure destruction, lacking consciousness and conscience—makes the characters wonder what sort of world they live in, whether God cares about them at all, and whether they are fundamentally in conflict with the world around them. In the face of the hurricane, Janie and the other characters wonder how they can possibly survive in a world filled with such chaos and pain.

SUMMARY & ANALYSIS

CHAPTERS 1–2

SUMMARY: CHAPTER 1

> *[T]he dream is the truth. Then they act and do things accordingly.*
>
> *(See* QUOTATIONS, *p. 55)*

As the sun sets in a southern town, a mysterious woman trudges down the main road. The local residents, gathered on Pheoby Watson's porch, know her, and they note her muddy overalls with satisfaction. Clearly resentful, they talk about how she had previously left the town with a younger man and gleefully speculate that he left her for a younger woman and took her money. They envy her physical beauty, particularly her long, straight hair. She doesn't stop to talk to them, and they interpret her passing by as aloofness. Her name, it is revealed, is Janie Starks, and the fellow with whom she ran off is named Tea Cake.

Pheoby criticizes the other women on the porch for their malicious gossip and sticks up for Janie. She excuses herself and visits Janie's home, bringing Janie a plate of food. Janie laughs when Pheoby repeats the other women's speculations to her. Janie explains that she has returned alone because Tea Cake is gone but not for the reasons that the crowd on the porch assumes. She has returned from living with Tea Cake in the Everglades, she explains, because she can no longer be happy there. Pheoby doesn't understand what she means, so Janie begins to tell her story.

SUMMARY: CHAPTER 2

> *[T]he thousand sister-calyxes arch to meet the love embrace . . . the ecstatic shiver of the tree . . . So this was a marriage!*
>
> *(See* QUOTATIONS, *p. 56)*

Janie is raised by her grandmother, Nanny. She never meets her mother or her father. Janie and Nanny inhabit a house in the backyard of a white couple, Mr. and Mrs. Washburn. She plays with the Washburns' children and thinks that she herself is white until she sees a photograph of herself. The children at the black school mock Janie for living in a white couple's backyard and tease her about her derelict parents. They often remind her that Mr. Washburn's dogs hunted her father down after he got her mother pregnant, though they neglect to mention that he actually wanted to marry her. Nanny eventually buys some land and a house because she thinks that having their own place will be better for Janie.

When Janie is sixteen, she often sits under a blossoming pear tree, deeply moved by the images of fertile springtime. One day, caught up in the atmosphere of her budding sexuality, she kisses a local boy named Johnny Taylor. Nanny catches Janie with Johnny and decides to marry Janie off to Logan Killicks, a wealthy middle-aged farmer. She wants to see Janie in a secure situation, which Logan Killicks can provide, before she dies. She says that black women are the mules of the world and that she doesn't want Janie to be a mule.

Janie protests, and Nanny recounts to her the hardships that she has experienced. Nanny was born into slavery. She was raped by her master and, a week after her daughter Leafy was born, her master went to fight during the last days of the Civil War. The master's wife was furious to see that Leafy had gray eyes and light hair and thus was obviously her husband's daughter. She planned to have Nanny viciously whipped and to sell Leafy once she was a month old. Nanny escaped with her baby and the two hid in the swamps until the war was over. Afterward, Nanny began working for the Washburns. Her dreams of a better life for Leafy ended when Leafy was raped by her schoolteacher. After giving birth to Janie, Leafy went out drinking every night and eventually ran off. Nanny transferred her hopes to Janie.

ANALYSIS: CHAPTERS 1–2

Their Eyes Were Watching God begins at the end of the story: we first see Janie after she has already grown old, concluded the adventures that she will relate, and been "tuh de horizon and back." Her story then spins out of her own mouth as she sits talking to Pheoby. From the very beginning of the book, then, language plays a crucial role; the book is framed more as an act of telling than of writing. Even before Janie speaks, we hear the murmur of the gossips on the porch: "A mood come alive. Words walking without masters." Throughout the book, speech, or more accurately, the control of language, proves crucially important. These first chapters introduce the important and complex role that language and speech will play throughout the novel.

One of the most commented-upon aspects of the novel is Hurston's split style of narrative. The book begins in an omniscient, third-person narrator's voice, one that is decidedly literary and intellectual, full of metaphors, figurative language, and other poetic devices. This voice anchors the entire novel and is clearly separate from Janie's voice. Hurston splits the narrative between this voice and long passages of dialogue uninterrupted by any comment from the narrator. These passages are marked by their highly colloquial language, colorful folksy aphorisms ("Unless you see de fur, a mink skin ain't no different from a coon hide"), and avoidance of Standard Written English. These unusual passages celebrate a rich folk tradition that is not often expressed on the page.

The oscillation between Standard Written English and Black Vernacular English mirrors one of the novel's central themes: the importance of controlling language. Throughout the book, we see Janie struggle with her own voice and control of language. As Gates writes in an afterword included in most modern editions of the book, Hurston views the "search for voice" as the defining quest of one's lifetime. The divided style of narration, however, suggests that the quest is complicated and lacks a singular resolution. Gates argues, "Hurston uses the two voices in her text to celebrate the psychological fragmentation of both modernity and of the black American . . . [H]ers is a rhetoric of division, rather than a fiction of psychological or cultural unity." Against this division, though, Hurston, in subtle ways, opens lines of communication between the two narrative styles. The third-person narrator is a voice that, while different from Janie's, partakes of figures and experiences in Janie's world. Hurston colors the narrator's sophisticated prose with colloquialisms, like the "Now" that opens the novel's second paragraph, nature metaphors, and a tone that reveals that the narrator delights in storytelling as much as any of the characters. Because of these qualities, the narrative voice is more than just the absence of dialect; the narrator has a personality that is related, though not identical, to those of the characters. Hurston's affection for black folklore and dialect is evident not only in its raw presentation in dialogue form but also in the traces it leaves on her high prose. The subtlety of the traces allows her to integrate the widely divergent styles into an aesthetic whole; the styles remain in tension but can speak to one another.

In Chapter Two, an important symbol is introduced: Janie's moment under the pear tree is a defining moment in her life and one that is referenced throughout the book. This experience relates symbolically to several themes: most obviously, Janie resonates with the sexuality of the springtime moment, and for the rest of the book, the pear tree serves as her standard of sexual and emotional fulfillment. At first glance, the tree seems to mirror traditional gender stereotypes: the tree (the female) waits passively for the aggressive male bee who penetrates its blossoms. But Hurston's careful language tweaks stereotypical notions of the female role: "the thousand sister calyxes arch to meet the love embrace and the ecstatic shiver of the tree. . . ." Although the tree waits for the arrival of the bee, the love embrace is *reciprocal*. From the opening passage of the book, it is clear that men and women are seen as fundamentally different. Janie doesn't want a male identity but rather a female one to parallel a male one; in the natural world, male and female impulses complement each other, creating a perfect union in a mutual embrace. Each gives the other what the other needs but does not yet possess. This ideal of love and fulfillment is at the center of Janie's quest throughout the book.

CHAPTERS 3–4

SUMMARY: CHAPTER 3

As Janie prepares for her marriage to Logan, she understands that she doesn't love him but assumes that after marriage, love will come naturally, as Nanny has been telling her. The wedding is a big, festive affair, but two months later, Janie visits Nanny to ask for advice; she fears that she will never love Logan. Nanny berates Janie for not appreciating Logan's wealth and status. She sends Janie on her way, again telling her that, in time, she will develop feelings for Logan. After Janie leaves, Nanny prays to God to care for Janie, saying that she, Nanny, has done the best that she could. A month later, she dies. A year passes, and Janie still feels no love for Logan and becomes even more disillusioned.

SUMMARY: CHAPTER 4

Logan pampers Janie less and tries to get her to perform manual labor, claiming that she is spoiled. One day, he leaves to buy a second mule so that Janie can help him work in the fields. While Logan is getting the mule, Janie spies a good-looking, sharply dressed stranger ambling down the road. She catches his eye and flirts a while with him; his name is Joe Starks, a smooth-tongued, stylish man with grand ambitions. He tells her that he is from Georgia, that he has saved up a lot of money, and that he has come down to Florida to move to a new town that is being built and run by blacks. He lingers around the town for a while and every day he and Janie meet secretly. He dazzles her with his big dreams, and Janie's hopes for love come alive again. He asks her to call him "Jody," a nickname that she has created for him. Finally, after about two weeks of clandestine flirtation, he says that he wants her to leave Logan and marry him.

That night, Janie and Logan fight. He again calls her spoiled and she mentions the possibility of running off. Feeling threatened, Logan responds desperately by insulting and belittling Janie. The next morning, they argue more. Logan orders her to help with the farm work; Janie says that he expects her to worship him but that she never will. Logan then breaks down, cursing her and sobbing. Afterward, Janie leaves to meet Jody at an agreed-upon time and place. They marry at the first opportunity and set out for the new town.

ANALYSIS: CHAPTERS 3–4

The conversation between Janie and Nanny in Chapter 3 neatly demonstrates the difference between their respective worldviews. For Nanny, relationships are a matter of pragmatism: Logan Killicks makes a good husband because he is well-off, honest, and hard-working. In a harsh world, he offers shelter and physical security. As Janie later realizes, in Chapter 12, it makes sense that a former slave like Nanny would have such a perspective. Her life has been one of poverty and hardship, with any hope of material advancement dashed by the color of her skin. Logan Killicks, a successful farmer who owns his own land, represents an ideal that she could only dream of when she was Janie's age.

But Janie clearly wants something more. She is searching for a deeper kind of fulfillment, one that offers both physical passion and emotional connection. Both the physical and emotional are important to Janie and inseparable from her idea of love. When explaining why she doesn't love Logan, she first mentions how ugly she thinks he is. She then mentions how he doesn't speak beautifully to her. She feels no connection to him—neither physical, nor emotional, nor intellectual.

Jody, on the other hand, seems to offer something more: he "spoke for far horizon." Throughout the book, the horizon is an important symbol. It represents imagination and limitless possibility, the type of life that Janie wants as opposed to the one that she has. It also represents the boundary of the natural world, the border of God's kingdom: "Janie knew that God tore down the old world every evening and built a new one by sun-up. It was wonderful to see it take form with the sun and emerge from the gray dust of its making." What lies beyond the horizon remains unclear; Janie doesn't know what to expect of Jody and the new life that he offers her. In fact, she is only certain of what he *doesn't* offer: "he did not represent sun-up and pollen and blooming trees. . . ." These are the figures of Janie's youthful romantic desires; she is willing to abandon or compromise these desires in exchange for the possibility of change.

Jody exudes possibility and freedom because he, unlike Logan, who is solid and dependable but dull and mule-like, bursts with ambition and power. Power, particularly the type of power expressed by Jody, is a crucial theme throughout the book. He talks about the future, travel, and conquest; to Janie, these ideas seem like ways to reach the far horizon. For the remainder of his time in the book, Jody Starks stands as a symbol of masculine aggression and power; he attempts to purchase, control, and dominate the world around him. As we later see, Jody's manner of interacting with the world fails to translate into secure happiness and fulfillment for Janie. At this point, though, she is dazzled by the power Jody offers and believes that it can grant her a better life.

CHAPTER 5

SUMMARY

Jody and Janie arrive in the Florida town to find that it consists of little more than a dozen shacks. Jody introduces himself to two men, Lee Coker and Amos Hicks, and asks to see the mayor; the men reply that there is none. Jody moves over to a porch to chat with a group of the townspeople, who tell him that the town's name is Eatonville. After hearing that Eatonville contains only fifty acres, Jody makes a big show of paying cash for an additional two hundred acres from Captain Eaton, one of the donors of Eatonville's existing land. Hicks stays behind to flirt—unsuccessfully—with Janie. Later, Coker teases Hicks because all the other men know that they can't lure a woman like Janie away from an ambitious, powerful, moneyed man like Jody.

After buying the land, Jody announces his plans to build a store and a post office and calls a town meeting. A man named Tony Taylor is technically chairman of the assembly, but Jody does all the talking. Jody hires Coker and Taylor to build his store while the rest of the town clears roads and recruits new residents. Jody soon recovers the cost of the new land by selling lots to newcomers and opens a store. At his store, Jody is quickly named mayor, and for the occasion Taylor asks Janie to give a short speech. Jody prevents her from doing so, saying that wives shouldn't make speeches. His opinion angers Janie, but she remains silent.

After becoming mayor, Jody decides that the town needs a street lamp. He buys the lamp with his own money and then calls a town meeting to vote on whether or not the town should install it. Though some dissent, a majority vote approves the motion. After the lamp arrives, Jody puts it on display for a week, and it becomes a source of pride for the whole town. He organizes a big gathering for the lighting, complete with guests from surrounding areas and a feast. The party is a huge success, full of ceremony and dignity. Afterward, Janie hints that she wants to spend more time with Jody now that he has done so much work. He replies that he is just getting started.

After a while, Jody and the rest of the town start to grow apart from each other, and Janie, as the mayor's wife, becomes the object of both respect and jealousy. The townspeople envy Jody's elaborate new two-story house that makes the rest of the houses look like servants' quarters. Jody buys spittoons for both himself and Janie, making them both seem like aristocrats flaunting their wealth and station. Furthermore, Jody runs a man named Henry Pitts out of town when he catches Henry stealing some of his ribbon cane. The townspeople wonder how Janie gets along with such a domineering man; after all, they note, she has such beautiful hair, but he makes her tie it up in a rag when she is working in the store. Though Jody's wealth and authority arouse the envy and animosity of some residents, no one challenges him.

SUMMARY & ANALYSIS

ANALYSIS

This chapter explores the masculine power that Jody Starks embodies. His political and economic conquest of the town recalls the opening passage of the book about "Ships at a distance." Jody is one of the few characters whose ship does come in, but his success is more of a curse than a blessing. His flaunting of his wealth and power alienates the townspeople. He appears to them as a darker version of the white master whom they thought they had escaped. His megalomania extends beyond social superiority to a need to play god, as the lamp lighting ceremony demonstrates. His words at the end of his speech, "let it shine, let it shine, let it shine," refer to a gospel hymn about Jesus as the Light of the World. Jody wants his light, the light that he bought, built, and put in place, to stand for the sun and, by extension, God himself. These words also hearken back to the Bible's account of creation, in which God says, "Let there be light" (Genesis 1:3). Jody's money and ambition give him power over the rest of the town, and he exploits this advantage to position himself as superior to the rest of the town. Such *hubris,* or presumptuousness, situates Jody in a classical scheme as one bound to fall.

Janie experiences the brunt of Jody's domineering nature. Jody never accepts Janie for what she is; instead, he tries to shape her into his image of the type of woman that he wants. She gets her first taste of his need to control her when he prevents her from making a speech after he is named mayor. Here, in particular, control is intertwined with language and speech: to allow Janie to speak would be to allow her to assert her identity in her own words. Forcing Janie to hide her hair is another way that Jody tries to control her. As hinted in Chapter 1, Janie's hair is an essential aspect of her identity and speaks to the strength of her person. Her hair's straightness signifies whiteness and therefore marks her as different from the rest of her community (and even marks her parents as deviant). Furthermore, its beauty and sensuousness denote the sexual nature of her being. Jody, in order to achieve complete control over Janie, must suppress this sexuality. Because he doesn't want her to inspire lust in other men and is "skeered some de rest of us mens might touch it round dat store," he orders her to wear her hair up in rags. Another man's interest in Janie would challenge or insult his authority.

Though Janie's hair exudes feminine sexuality and is a locus of contestation among the men, it also has a masculine quality. Because of its shape, Janie's braided hair is clearly a phallic symbol. This phallic symbolism is typical of Hurston's deconstruction of traditional categories of representation. In Janie's hair, feminine beauty, traditionally the object of male desire and aggression, acquires power and becomes the acting agent. Janie's hair represents the power that she wields—her refusal (in later chapters) to be dominated by men and her refusal to obey traditional notions of female submission to male desire.

CHAPTER 6

> *[Nature]'s de strongest thing dat God ever made, now.*
> *Fact is it's de onliest thing God every made.*
>   *(See* QUOTATIONS, *p. 57)*

Janie dislikes the business of running the store but loves that people sit on its porch and talk all day telling colorful, exaggerated stories. The men love teasing a man named Matt Bonner about his over-worked, underfed, bad-tempered mule. They make jokes about how sorry the mule looks and needle Matt about how careless and cruel he is toward the animal. Despite Janie's interest in these stories, Jody doesn't allow her to sit outside, saying that she's too good to interact with "trashy people." But most annoying to Janie of all, Jody orders her to wear a head-rag because it makes him jealous to see other men look at her long hair, though he never reveals his motives to Janie.

One day, Matt Bonner's mule runs away, and some of the towns-men find it outside the store. They irritate the mule for fun, and Janie mutters her disapproval of their cruelty. Unbeknownst to her, Jody is standing nearby and hears her complaint. He buys the mule for five dollars so that the poor beast can rest for once in his life. Every-one considers Jody's liberation of the mule very noble, comparing it to Abraham Lincoln's emancipation of northern slaves. The animal becomes a source of pride for the town and the subject of even more tall tales. After it dies, Jody convenes a mock funeral, which becomes a festive event for the entire town. But Jody refuses to allow Janie to attend, saying it would be improper for a woman of her sta-tus. After the funeral, vultures descend on the animal's carcass.

At the store, Jody and Janie argue. She accuses him of being no fun and he argues that he is just being responsible. Although she dis-agrees, she decides to hold her tongue. On the porch, meanwhile, Sam Watson (Pheoby's husband) and Lige Moss hold a humorous philosophical debate. They argue about whether natural instinct or a learned sense of caution keeps men away from hot stoves. The good-spirited argument gets intense and Jody decides to join it, leav-ing his delivery boy Hezekiah Potts in charge of the store. The con-versation shifts to a discussion of the Sinclair gas station in town but then becomes a playful performance of machismo and flirtation as several of the town's women parade by. Janie is enjoying the fun when Jody orders her back in the store to wait on one of the women.

When Janie cannot find any pig's feet for another customer, Jody grows angry and accuses her of incompetence. Instead of fighting back, Janie remains silent. But as time goes on, her resentment builds. She feels the spark go out of their sex life and the spirit of love leave their marriage. One day, seven years after they met, Jody slaps her after a disastrous dinner. Still, Janie doesn't express her anger; she decides to maintain an exterior of silent respect while keeping her dreams and emotions inside.

But later that day, Janie goes to the store. There, she finds Tony Robbins's wife begging Jody for a little meat for her family. Jody gives her a small piece and adds the cost to Tony's account. The men on the porch mutter that they would never allow their wives to embarrass them like that, especially since her husband had spent so much money on her. Janie finally cannot resist speaking up, scolding the men and saying that they don't know as much about women as they think they do. She points out that it is easy to act big and tough when women and chickens are the only things around to subdue. Jody tells her to be quiet and orders her to fetch him a checkerboard.

ANALYSIS

Chapter 6 serves two chief functions: it further explores Janie and Jody's relationship, particularly his need for control, and it examines the strong sense of community in Eatonville, particularly the way language nurtures this sense of community. Both of these issues relate to Janie's continuing quest to find herself and a sense of meaning and purpose. Initially drawn to Jody because of his ambition, and thinking that she would achieve her dreams through him, Janie learns, in this chapter, that Jody's power only restricts her. On the other hand, by experiencing the richness of life in Eatonville, in particular the rich folk traditions of conversation, Janie begins to see how she might live the life that she so desires.

Jody continues to exert the same kind of control over Janie that he does in Chapter 5. It is important to note, however, that Jody is not an evil character. Indeed, there are no true antagonists in the book, and evil is not manifested in specific individuals. Jody doesn't cause pain for its own sake; rather, pain results for Janie as a result of the way that Jody acts—according to the rules that make sense to him, misguided though they are. He is living the only way he knows how. In his heart, he does not intend to hurt people, but his unfailing belief in a social hierarchy dominated by wealthy males inevitably hurts those around him.

That Jody is not fundamentally evil manifests itself in the episode with Matt Bonner's mule. Jody's purchase of the animal is a tender moment: unbeknownst to Janie, he spares the animal in order to please her. It is a noble display of power both because it frees the mule from cruelty and because it is meant to please Janie. But even in moments such as this one, Jody's relationship to Janie still operates according to an imbalanced power dynamic. Though this incident is not a matter of anger or ambition but rather tender kindness, he can demonstrate this kindness only by means of money. He is unable or unwilling to interact on equal terms with Janie; he uses his purchasing power to express his emotions.

Furthermore, we get the sense that perhaps Jody's actions are not so noble. One can argue that he senses Janie slipping away from him and that he intends the act to woo her back under his dominion. Indeed, he is praised for his compassion, and the comparison to Lincoln only feeds Jody's haughty sense of himself—the same egotism with which he first attracts Janie. In refusing to allow Janie to attend the mule's funeral, Jody again prioritizes issues of decorum over Janie's happiness; he would rather keep up the appearance of his wife as a perfect lady than indulge her emotions. The unromantic, commonplace descent of the vultures upon the mule's carcass after the funeral seems to testify, if not to the shallowness of Jody's motivations, then to his inability to express himself suitably.

Hurston again uses two different narrative devices to differentiate between the realm of Janie and Jody's relationship and that of the community. The third-person omniscient narrator describes Janie's life in the store: except for her outburst at the end, she remains silent, and the narrator tells us her story. But in the lengthy passages of dialogue, we are brought deeper into the world of the novel: instead of being told a story, we are actually being *shown* a world. As Henry Louis Gates Jr. points out in his essay *"Their Eyes Were Watching God:* Hurston and the Speakerly Text," we experience the full richness of these conversations because the characters speak for themselves. Only rarely does the narrator interrupt to tell us something about the scene.

Sam Watson and Lige Moss's conversation about the role of nature in the world strikes at the heart of the novel's central theme: the relationship between humans and the world around them. The porch conversation is, in modern terms, a debate over nature versus nurture: whether we are as we are because of what we are born with (nature) or what we are taught (nurture). Sam Watson's comment that "[God] made nature and nature made everything else" resonates throughout the novel, particularly at the climax, when all of the characters find themselves at the mercy of nature. Janie is attracted to these conversations because of the warm human connection that they offer and their organic, humorous approach to the questions that are at the center of her journey to the horizon. Her outburst at the end of the chapter represents an attempt to break out from Jody's silencing control and join the world of the porch.

CHAPTERS 7–8

SUMMARY: CHAPTER 7

As the years pass, Janie grows more and more defeated. She silently submits to Jody's imperious nature and performs her duties while ignoring her emotions. She considers running away but doubts that she can find refuge anywhere, feeling that she has grown unattractive. She feels her spirit detach from her body; she watches herself work at the store and submit to Jody while her mind is really elsewhere. This detachment allows her to accept stoically a life that she has grown to hate.

One day, Janie notices that Jody has begun to look quite old. He has trouble moving around and his body bulges and sags. Jody, too, seems aware of this physical change, and he pesters Janie about her age and appearance, attempting to get her to worry about her own appearance and ignore his. But Janie sees through his ploy. She realizes how ugly and old he feels.

Jody keeps deteriorating and, as a result, his verbal attacks become more vicious and frequent. One day, Janie makes a clumsy mistake while cutting a plug of tobacco for a customer. Jody begins berating her in front of the store crowd, not only mocking her incompetence but also insulting her looks. Janie finally releases her pent-up aggression. She insults his sagging body and declares that he looks like "de change uh life" when naked. The force of the insult stuns the men on the porch. Jody feels impotent, his reputation in the town diminished and his power vanishing. He lashes out in a blind rage, fiercely hitting Janie and driving her from the store.

SUMMARY: CHAPTER 8

After the confrontation, Jody moves into another room in the house. His health keeps deteriorating and he grows desperate, consulting with quacks who promise miracle cures. He avoids contact with Janie and stops eating her cooking. Janie learns from Pheoby that there is a rumor around town that Janie is trying to poison Jody for revenge. Nevertheless, Janie sends for a real doctor from Orlando. The doctor examines Jody and determines that his kidneys have stopped working and that he will soon die.

Janie begins to pity Jody and wants to see him one last time. Jody refuses, but Janie decides that it will soon be too late, so she enters his room. He is cold and distant, and their conversation quickly deteriorates into an argument. He says that she never appreciated all that he did for her; she responds that he never let her express her emotions. She then tells him that he is dying and Jody finally realizes the truth. He breaks down, releases one long, anguished sob, and begs Janie not to tell him such things. Nevertheless, she berates him, accusing him of tyranny and egotism. She adds that he was always trying to change her and was never satisfied with who she really was.

Jody pleads with Janie to stop but she continues. She sees that he is struggling with death and is filled with pity. He dies, and she thinks about all the time that has passed since she met him. She looks in a mirror and sees that she has aged but is still beautiful. She rips off her head-rag, freeing her imprisoned hair, but then realizes that she must appear to be mourning. She ties it back up, assumes a mask of sadness, and yells out the window that Jody has died.

ANALYSIS: CHAPTERS 7–8

These two chapters focus on the disintegration of Jody and Janie's marriage, culminating in Jody's death. Janie's interest in the marriage has already waned by this point. She loses hope when it becomes clear that her relationship to Jody will not realize her dreams. Jody, on the other hand, loses everything, including the will to live, as soon as he loses the ability to exert control. Despite their obvious differences, Jody and Janie's situations are, in a way, similar. Both realize that they have constructed lives that have not delivered the fulfillment that they expected. But Janie is able to survive her disillusionment and, by the end of Chapter Eight, has begun to once again head in the direction of her dreams. Jody, however, doesn't survive; in part, his destruction results from Janie's reassertion of herself.

In Chapter 6 we see how intimately Jody's control is related to language. He uses language to belittle Janie while at the same time forcing her to remain silent. The one-sidedness of this dynamic is the only real tool left with which Jody can preserve the imbalance of power in his relationship with Janie. Jody tries to use his control of discourse to compensate for his physical deterioration and ultimate inability to control the world. His insults attempt to reshape the world around him by incorrectly describing Janie's appearance while ignoring his own.

Janie's two outbursts further underscore the importance of language. When she speaks, she asserts herself and her own power; this assertion, of course, deeply troubles Jody. Janie's sharp retort in Chapter 7 about Jody's feebleness completely shatters Jody's misconceptions about the extent of his power: he is "robbed . . . of his illusion of irresistible maleness." Janie has reversed their situations. Earlier, Jody prevents her from speaking and asserting her identity; now, he himself is left without a voice: "Joe Starks didn't know the words for all this, but he knew the feeling." Stung by words, shown the limitations of his power, and robbed of his ability to speak, Jody breaks down. He resorts to physical violence—a display of beastliness—because his lofty aura has dissipated completely.

Jody's disintegration is completed in Chapter 8, and, once again, he is undone by the power of Janie's speech. She finally lashes out at him in full, expressing her feelings and criticizing his faults. Janie compromises the source of Jody's power—his assumed superiority—rendering him impotent and weak. It is no coincidence that he dies as Janie finishes her scolding speech.

Janie's first act of liberation after Jody's death is to release her hair from the shackles of the head-rag. She reasserts her identity as beautiful and arousing woman—an identity that Jody has denied her by trying to suppress her sex appeal and making comments about her aging appearance. Her braid again functions as a phallic symbol, representing her potency and strength. Jody has kept Janie's power tied up, but now she is free and can release it. But Janie's act of tying her hair back up demonstrates that she understands that the community will judge her if she appears so carefree; unlike Jody, who exerts his authority without regard for others, Janie wields her power with restraint.

CHAPTERS 9–10

SUMMARY: CHAPTER 9

After Jody's elaborate funeral, Janie begins her period of mourning. On the inside she feels released and joyous, but she maintains a sad face for the outside world. The only noticeable change is that she begins wearing her hair in a long braid again, having burned all of her head rags. Now that she is alone, she begins to examine her feelings and realizes that she hates Nanny for the values with which Nanny raised her. Nanny taught her to seek superficial prizes such as wealth, security, and status instead of chasing her dreams.

Soon, men begin approaching Janie; as an attractive and wealthy woman, she would make quite a prize. Despite these constant advances, Janie's six months of mourning pass without any suitor making progress. Janie's newfound freedom and independence make her happy and she has no desire to become tied down to another man. Her only source of unhappiness is the store, which she continues to run. She feels Jody's domineering presence everywhere. Eventually Hezekiah Potts begins to imitate Jody, but his mimicry is only amusing, not threatening. As per custom, Janie begins wearing white after six months, supposedly signaling her availability for suitors. But she continues to rebuff all advances and confides to Pheoby that she loves her new independence. Pheoby responds that the townspeople will think that she isn't sad that Jody is dead. Janie replies that she doesn't care what the town thinks because she shouldn't pretend to be sad if she isn't.

SUMMARY: CHAPTER 10

One day, Hezekiah leaves the store early to go to a baseball game. Janie decides to close up early, since most of the town is at the game. But before she can do so, a tall stranger enters the store. He buys cigarettes from her and then begins making flirtatious small talk, making her laugh with his jokes. He invites her to play checkers, which thrills her; no man has ever respected her enough to ask her to play checkers. She notices his good looks and shapely body.

Janie and the stranger play a good-natured game and continue their flirtation. Afterward, they chat some more and Janie asks him how he plans to get home. He answers that he always finds a way home, even if that requires sneaking onto a train illegally. She finally asks his name, and he replies that it is Vergible Woods but that everyone calls him Tea Cake. He pretends to leave but makes Janie laugh with a playful, imaginative joke, and he stays around. They continue to joke and laugh until the store fills with people returning from the game, and they talk until everyone goes home for the night. He helps her lock up the store, walks her to her porch, and chastely bids her good night.

ANALYSIS: CHAPTERS 9–10

Chapters 9 and 10 mark the beginning of Janie's liberation. First, she learns how to be alone. Then, Tea Cake's arrival brings her to a second stage in her development, as she begins to see what kind of relationship she wants and how it will help her attain her dreams. Throughout Chapter 9, Janie brims with independence and strength. We see her with her hair down, the symbol of her potency free and unfettered. Additionally, this chapter is full of Janie's voice. Unlike the previous chapters, in which Jody forcibly keeps her silent, Janie is now full of conversation: she talks to Ike Green, Hezekiah, and Pheoby, all the while asserting her own desires.

As Janie enjoys her newfound freedom of speech, she becomes more introspective and self-aware. In previous chapters, Janie distances herself from her emotions in order to survive with Jody. Now, however, she confronts feelings that have lain dormant for almost two decades. She realizes, somewhat to our surprise, that she hates her grandmother for raising her according to a flawed belief system that values materialism and social status. Janie understands that while people are what matter to her, she had been raised to value things. Nevertheless, she has a mature enough understanding of life not to blame Nanny; she understands that Nanny impressed these values upon her out of love. As with Jody, evil is localized not so much in a person as in a broader set of beliefs. Nanny is not really a villain; she is merely misguided by a flawed way of looking at the world.

With Tea Cake, an entirely new worldview enters the story. Tea Cake clearly respects Janie for who she is and wants to engage her in a substantive manner. He converses with her and plays checkers with her—both activities that grant equal status to the participants. The substantial space that Hurston devotes to their conversation contrasts with Janie's first meeting with Jody in Chapter 4, when he charms and overwhelms her with his smooth talking. Foreshadowing the lack of meaningful contact to come in their relationship, Janie's first conversation with Jody is brief. Their subsequent flirtations are not presented directly but instead glossed over by the narration: "Every day after that they managed . . . to talk. . . ." When Tea Cake and Janie first meet, on the other hand, they fill several pages with real dialogue, hinting at the potential richness of their relationship.

Furthermore, Tea Cake exhibits a creativity that is immensely appealing to Janie. He makes her laugh with fanciful, imaginative jokes: pretending to hide behind imaginary lampposts, talking to invisible companions, making puns and creative wordplays. Tea Cake's show of creativity contrasts with Jody's penchant for consumption. Whereas Jody lives to consume and has materialistic goals involving power and status that he displays with objects like fancy spittoons, Tea Cake, as his creativity demonstrates, is concerned with things beyond material life. By this point in the novel, Janie has realized that her quest for the horizon involves a pursuit of the mystical and unknowable, mysteries that Jody's materialistic worldview could never approach. Through his respect for her and his vibrancy, Tea Cake seems to Janie the man who will complement her and take her toward the horizon for which she longs.

CHAPTERS 11–12

SUMMARY: CHAPTER 11

Tea Cake doesn't come back for a week, and Janie, thinking that he is taking advantage of her wealth, decides to be rude to him when he shows up. But when he finally comes by, his fanciful joking—he pretends to play an imaginary guitar—immediately makes Janie smile. They flirt and play checkers again, and then Tea Cake walks Janie home. They sit on her porch and talk for hours, eating cake and drinking fresh lemonade. As late as it is, Tea Cake proposes that they go fishing. They stay out the rest of the night at the lake, and in the morning, Janie has to sneak Tea Cake out of town to avoid gossip. She loves the impetuous adventure of the whole evening.

The next day, Hezekiah tells Janie that Tea Cake is too low for a woman like her; Janie, however, doesn't care. Tea Cake returns that night and they eat a dinner of fresh fish. Afterward, Janie falls asleep in Tea Cake's lap and wakes up to find him brushing her hair. They talk for a while, and Tea Cake says that he fears that Janie thinks that he is a scoundrel. Janie tells him that she likes him, but as a good friend not a lover. Crushed, Tea Cake says that he feels more strongly about her than she apparently does about him. Janie doesn't believe him, thinking that he can't possibly be attracted to someone so much older than him. She tells him that he will feel different in the morning. Tea Cake leaves abruptly.

The next day, Janie anxiously frets about Tea Cake, who doesn't return. The day after that, however, he wakes her up by knocking on her door. He says that he has to leave for work but that he wanted to let her know that his feelings for her are real. That night, Janie finds Tea Cake waiting for her in her hammock. They eat dinner and he spends the night. The next morning, he leaves. Janie is again filled with desperate fears that Tea Cake has simply taken advantage of her. But he returns after three days, driving a beat-up car, and says that he wants to make their relationship public; he bought the car because he wants to take her to the big town picnic.

SUMMARY: CHAPTER 12

After the picnic, Tea Cake and Janie become the topic of scandalous gossip. The town doesn't approve of the revered mayor's widow dating a poor, younger man. Sam Watson convinces Pheoby to talk to Janie so that she doesn't end up like Ms. Tyler, an old widow who was cheated by a younger man. Pheoby tells Janie that Tea Cake is too low for her, but Janie replies that while Jody wanted her to act pretentious and high-class, Tea Cake treats her as she wants to be treated. Pheoby warns that Tea Cake may be using her for her money and tells Janie that she has stopped mourning for Jody too soon. Janie dismisses these admonitions, saying she shouldn't mourn if she is not sad. Janie then reveals that she plans to sell the store, leave town, and marry Tea Cake. She explains that she doesn't want the town to compare Tea Cake to Jody. She also says that she has lived her grandmother's way and now wants to live her own way. She adds that augmented status seemed like the ultimate achievement to a former slave like Nanny but that she, Janie, is searching for something deeper. Pheoby cautions her once more to be careful with Tea Cake, but then the two women laugh and share in Janie's newfound happiness.

ANALYSIS: CHAPTERS 11–12

Chapter 11 deepens our understanding of Janie's attraction to Tea Cake. By the end of this chapter, Janie has begun to see him in mystical terms and has developed a conscious sense that he is the partner that she needs in order to travel to the horizon. Chapter 12 contrasts Janie's attachment to Tea Cake with her relationship to the town as a whole and further explores Janie's personal growth. Through her conversation with Pheoby Watson, we see that Janie has a clearer idea now than ever before of who she is and what she wants.

In Chapter 12, we see how Janie's relationship with Tea Cake has superceded her desire to interact with the community around her. In Chapter 6, when Janie hungers to join the world of the porch-talkers, the community life of the town seems to offer the interaction missing from her isolated life with Jody. But Tea Cake now shows her an intimacy that she considers far more valuable. Whereas, earlier, the opinion of the town means a great deal to Janie, she has now gained such an amount of self-confidence and has been exposed to such a fulfilling relationship that she is able to dismiss the petty gossip of the town around her. The community, on the other hand, resents Janie and Tea Cake's relationship precisely because it replaces the intimacy that the community offers; with Tea Cake, Janie has found a connection much deeper and truer than that which the porch offers.

Throughout Chapter 12, we witness how much Janie has matured since her relationship with Jody. During her conversation with Pheoby, she is able to articulate complex, previously inexpressible ideas and emotions. In Chapter 9, Janie bluntly states that she hates her grandmother. In Chapter 12, she offers a more nuanced perspective—she understands that Nanny's distorted priorities were a product of the harsh life that she experienced as a slave. Again we see that antagonism is not located in a particular person but is rather manifested in harmful systems of beliefs. In this case, Nanny was the victim of slavery and Janie, in turn, was the victim of the mindset that Nanny's experience shaped in Nanny. Here, we see that large forces, such as cultural forces and environmental circumstances, not particular people, are the sources of pain. Janie's newfound sympathy for her grandmother represents another step toward attaining her goal: she now sees from where she has come and why she was unhappy with Jody. She realizes that her quest is a spiritual one, searching for more than mere materialism.

It is significant that all of these revelations come in the course of conversation; Hurston maintains her emphasis on speech interaction. Janie's quest for self-discovery is literally a quest to find her own voice. Thus, it is important to note her description of Tea Cake's meaning to her: "He done taught me the maiden language all over." Janie's love for Tea Cake is framed in terms of *language*: in helping her find her voice, he has given her the tools to understand her inner desires. Through her reciprocally rewarding relationship with Tea Cake, Janie has finally begun to take real steps toward the horizon.

CHAPTERS 13–14

SUMMARY: CHAPTER 13

Janie leaves Eatonville and meets Tea Cake in Jacksonville, where they marry. Still wary of being ripped off, Janie doesn't tell Tea Cake about the two hundred dollars that she has pinned inside her shirt. A week later, Tea Cake leaves early, saying that he is just running to get fish for breakfast. He doesn't come back, and Janie discovers that her money is missing. She spends the day thinking about Ms. Tyler, the widow in Eatonville who had been ripped off by a charming rascal named Who Flung. But Tea Cake returns later that night to a still-distraught Janie. He explains that a wave of excitement came over him when he saw the money; he spent it all on a big chicken and macaroni dinner for his fellow railroad workers. It turned into a raucous party, full of music and fighting. Janie is insulted that Tea Cake didn't invite her, but Tea Cake further explains that he was worried that Janie might think that his crowd was too low class. Janie says that from now on, she wants to enjoy everything that he does.

Tea Cake then promises to reimburse Janie. He claims to be a great gambler and goes off Saturday night to play dice and cards. Again, he disappears for a while and Janie frets. Around daybreak he returns. He got hurt the previous night, cut with a razor by an angry loser, but he won three hundred and twenty-two dollars. Janie, who now trusts Tea Cake, tells him about the twelve hundred dollars that she has in the bank. Tea Cake announces that she will never have to touch it, that he will provide for her, and that they will leave for "the muck" (the Everglades), where he will get work.

SUMMARY: CHAPTER 14

Janie, completely in love with Tea Cake, is overwhelmed by the rich fertile fields of the Everglades. Tea Cake is familiar with life in the muck and immediately gets them settled before the season's rush of migrant workers arrives. He plans to pick beans during the day and play guitar and roll dice at night. As the season begins, Tea Cake and Janie live a comfortable life. They plant beans, Tea Cake teaches

Janie how to shoot a gun, and they go hunting together. She eventually develops into a better shot than him.

The season soon gets underway. Poor transients pour into the muck in droves to farm the land; eventually, all the houses are taken and people camp out in the fields. At night, the Everglades are filled with wild energy as the cheap bars pulse with music and revelry. Tea Cake's house becomes a center of the community, a place where people hang out and listen to him play music. At first, Janie stays at home and cooks glorious meals, but soon Tea Cake gets lonely and begins cutting work to see her. Janie then decides to join him in the fields so that they can be together all day. Working in her overalls and sitting on the cabin stoop with the migrant workers, Janie laughs to herself about what the people in Eatonville would say if they could see her. She feels bad for the status-obsessed townspeople who cannot appreciate the folksy pleasure of sitting and jawing on the porch.

ANALYSIS: CHAPTERS 13–14

Up to this point, the relationship between Janie and Tea Cake has seemed almost too good to be true. Chapters 13 and 14, while continuing to demonstrate that their relationship is a good experience for Janie, raise some complex questions about Tea Cake's character. Their arrival in the Everglades is a moment of fulfillment for Janie as she finds herself surrounded by fertile nature. Overall, her experience is generally a fulfilling one. Nevertheless, Tea Cake manipulates her in subtle ways, raising, once again, the specter of male domination in her life.

Chapter 13 is marked by Tea Cake's cruel absences from Janie. Although Janie accepts his explanations, it is hard to believe that someone as intelligent as Tea Cake could be so careless only a week after his wedding. His departure to go gambling seems likewise strange and needlessly risky. Yet after all her suffering in this chapter, Janie is more in love with Tea Cake than before; she feels a complete, powerful, "self-crushing love." Tea Cake has become a personification of all that she wants; her dreams and Tea Cake have become one and the same. In literary terms, this is a kind of metonymy, or substitution: Tea Cake has enabled Janie to begin her quest and, in the process, has become the goal of her quest.

Tea Cake stokes Janie's desire by maintaining his distance from her. The old cliché "absence makes the heart grow fonder" is applicable; in more academic language, Janie's desire is predicated on a lack of what she wants most. Tea Cake seems to manipulate this lack to make Janie love him more. In Chapter 14, he achieves something neither Logan nor Jody is able to accomplish: getting Janie to work out of her own free will. Having already shown her the pain of separation from him in Chapter 13, Tea Cake plays on this memory to make her want to work in the fields. One can also argue, however, that Tea Cake's actions are not so manipulative. After all, part of his attractiveness stems from his wild, vivacious personality; perhaps his partying and gambling are simply manifestations of his character. Similarly, perhaps he is being genuine when he claims to be lonely during the day; neither the narrator nor Janie considers his intentions anything but honest.

In any case, it is important to remember that Tea Cake makes Janie genuinely happy. He continues to accord her respect and remains unthreatened by her empowerment. He teaches her to shoot a gun, another phallic object associated with masculine power, and remains undisturbed by the fact that she becomes more proficient than him. Unlike Jody, who forces Janie to conceal the masculine power that her hair embodies, Tea Cake encourages Janie's strength. Finally, Janie's time in the Everglades is filled with incredible richness. The long final paragraph of Chapter 14 is an exuberant celebration—once again using extended vernacular dialogue—of the folk life of the Everglades. She is closer than ever before to the ideal of the pear tree, leading a satisfying life within rich, fertile nature.

This nearing toward her dream is perhaps the reason that Janie sticks with Tea Cake despite his lapses in judgment. He treats her terribly at times, taking her presence for granted and dominating her emotions. Although he clearly loves and needs her, he certainly possesses her more than she possesses him. Yet Janie doesn't mind this inequality. This acceptance of inequality is related to the idea of gender differences postulated at the beginning of the novel. As becomes evident in subsequent chapters, Hurston implies that men have a fundamental need for possession that women lack. Because Tea Cake respects Janie so much, his occasional domination of her seems insignificant. In fact, it could be argued that Tea Cake's domineering personality is what enables Janie to grow. He pulls her down to the Everglades without any input from her and it becomes the most fulfilling experience of her life.

CHAPTERS 15–16

SUMMARY: CHAPTER 15

After a while in the muck, Janie begins to grow jealous of Nunkie, a chunky girl who flirts with Tea Cake in the fields. As the season goes on, Nunkie grows bolder and bolder and is always falling over Tea Cake and playfully touching him. One day, Janie gets distracted and then finds that Nunkie and Tea Cake have disappeared. Their friend Sop-de-Bottom tells Janie that Nunkie and Tea Cake are over in a patch of cane. Janie rushes over and finds them play-wrestling on the ground. Tea Cake explains that Nunkie stole his work tickets and coquettishly made him tussle for them. Nunkie flees, and when the couple returns home, Janie tries to beat Tea Cake. But he holds her off, and her wild anger transforms into wild passion. In bed the next morning, they both joke about what a foolish girl Nunkie is.

SUMMARY: CHAPTER 16

> *Through indiscriminate suffering men know fear ... the most divine emotion. . . . Half gods are worshipped in wine and flowers. Real gods require blood.*
> (See QUOTATIONS, p. 58)

The season ends, and Janie and Tea Cake decide to stay around for another year. During the off-season, there isn't much to do, so Janie spends more time socializing. She hangs out a little with the exotic Bahamians that live in the muck but spends most of her time with Mrs. Turner. Although she is black, Mrs. Turner, a funny-looking, conceited woman, talks all the time about the evils of black people. She loves whiteness and argues that black people are lazy and foolish and that they should try to "lighten up de race." She dislikes the dark-skinned Tea Cake and wants Janie to marry her light-skinned brother.

Tea Cake overhears a conversation between Janie and Mrs. Turner and tells Janie that he doesn't want Mrs. Turner around the house. He plans to visit Mr. Turner to tell him to keep his wife away, but when he meets the man on the street, Tea Cake finds that he is a depressed, passive man dominated by his wife and drained by the deaths of several of his children. He gets Janie to try to end her friendship with Mrs. Turner. Janie acts coldly toward Mrs. Turner, but the woman keeps visiting nonetheless. Mrs. Turners worships whiteness, and Janie, by virtue of her light skin and high-class demeanor, represents an ideal for her. She disapproves of Janie's marriage to Tea Cake, but her opinions matter little to them. The summer soon ends, and the busy season begins again.

ANALYSIS: CHAPTERS 15–16

The incident with Nunkie shows Janie's need for absolute monogamy with Tea Cake. Because he wholly possesses her, she cannot bear the thought that she does not wholly possess him. Although the previous chapters establish the inequalities in their relationship, this chapter reveals that Janie is not willing to compromise on important matters; their relationship must be reciprocal. It is interesting to see how this reciprocity is expressed. At the first moment of reconciliation—the steamy passion that follows their fight—they express themselves through their bodies. Speech, however, remains the key to Janie's strength and identity; despite their physical connection, Janie still needs Tea Cake to *tell* her that he doesn't love Nunkie.

Through Janie's interactions with Mrs. Turner, Chapter 16 provides the clearest perspective on issues of race in the novel. Many critics dismissed *Their Eyes Were Watching God* when it was first published because of its atypical discussion of race. At the time, most critics, black and white alike, expected a novel by a black author to deal with issues of race in stark, political terms. Hurston's presentation of race and racism, however, is nuanced and remarkably free of political diatribe. When discussing Hurston's perspective on race, one cannot underestimate the effect of Franz Boas and his anthropological outlook on her philosophy. Boas, considered one of the most important anthropologists of the 20th century, was Hurston's professor at Barnard College from 1925 to 1927. Instead of approaching race as a marker of innate difference and inferiority, he began to use anthropology to study race in cultural terms, discussing, for example, how ideas of racism circulate. Boas believed that race is not the fundamental truth about a person or group of people but rather a mere cultural construct that affects the perception of a specific person or group. Boas's perspective was the source of Hurston's iconoclastic depiction of racism: in the novel, racism is a mode of thought, capable of seducing white and black alike, and, as such, is a force larger than any particular person or group.

Indeed, the narrator attributes near cosmic significance to Mrs. Turner's racism. In her obsession with whiteness, she "like all the other believers had built an altar to the unattainable," the narrator reveals, which seems to be a comparison to Jody's materialism and thirst for power. This comparison destabilizes the gender conventions that Hurston posits at the opening of the novel: Mrs. Turner, as men do, watches a metaphorical "Ships at a distance." Hurston does not dogmatically bind herself to her own conception of gender differences. As Janie's hair can be both a site of feminine beauty and a phallic symbol, Mrs. Turner can worship false gods like male characters.

The narrator's meditation on Mrs. Turner's racism also occasions stylistic variation. When describing ordinary events, the narrator often employs language that resonates with the dialect of the novel's characters. The Chapter 16 sentence, "That is why she sought out Janie to friend with," for example, turns the noun "friend" into a verb and ends with a preposition, violating a convention of Standard Written English. Indeed, the narrator sounds like an educated Janie. This subtle incorporation of black dialect into the narrator's voice integrates the dialogue and narration into a workable whole: the narration and dialogue do use very different styles, but one can hear the echo of the dialogue in the narration, and this echo helps to glue the two styles together. In the discussion of Mrs. Turner's racism, however, the narrator's voice loses the folksy tone and flies off into omniscient, high poetry. Here, Hurston indulges her command of pithy, almost biblical language: "That was the mystery and mysteries are the chores of gods." The display is impressive, but the stronger the language becomes, the greater the strain between it and the narrator's other voice, which uses nouns as verbs and illustrates with barnyard metaphors. *Their Eyes Were Watching God* is framed as Janie's telling of a story, but words in the text like "insensate," "seraph," and "fanaticism" seem to resist such a context. These words and the poetic passages in which they occur do not sound like they were filtered through Janie's personality. The narration itself has two different styles. This difference is problematic if we expect the narrator to maintain one style. On the other hand, the novel self-consciously deals with the control of language and transgression of convention. Rigorous adherence to one style of narration may be as legitimate a target for transgression as traditional gender roles.

CHAPTERS 17–18

SUMMARY: CHAPTER 17

As the season begins, some familiar faces return and some new faces appear. Mrs. Turner brings her brother to town and Tea Cake, feeling threatened, beats Janie to show that he still controls her. He pampers her afterward, and Janie harbors no ill-will toward him. All the men are envious of his power over her.

On Saturdays, workers receive their pay, and many use their money to buy liquor. One particular Saturday, two men named Dick Sterrett and Coodemay get drunk and walk around the town making a ruckus. They end up at Mrs. Turner's restaurant, where Tea Cake and his crowd are eating. They get rowdy and a fight breaks out. Tea Cake tries to throw the two out and get on Mrs. Turner's good side, but his efforts only lead to further havoc. The restaurant gets trashed, and Mrs. Turner gets trampled and injured. She fumes at her husband for passively letting the roustabouts wreck her business.

SUMMARY: CHAPTER 18

> They sat in company with the others . . . They seemed to
> be staring at the dark, but their eyes were watching
> God.
>
> (See QUOTATIONS, p. 59)

One day, Janie sees several groups of Native Americans departing the Everglades for Palm Beach. She asks them why they are leaving and they respond that a hurricane is coming. The news spreads through the settlement and everyone begins watching anxiously. Over the next few days, more indigenous people leave and animals begin scurrying off in the same direction. Soon, workers begin leaving the town. Although he is offered a ride to higher ground, Tea Cake decides to stay. Several men who decide to stay gather at Tea Cake's house, and a party ensues. But as the storm whips up, all of the men leave for their own houses except a fellow named Motor Boat. That night and the next day, the storm builds in the distance and the gigantic Lake Okechobee begins to roil. The three of them wait out the storm in the shanty with "their eyes . . . watching God."

Tea Cake says that he bets Janie wishes that she had stayed in her big house in Eatonville, but she replies that she doesn't care what happens as long as they remain together. He goes outside and sees that a serious flood has begun. They decide to flee. They gather up some essential papers and, arms locked against the wind, Tea Cake, Janie, and Motor Boat head east to higher ground.

The three look behind them and see that the Okechobee's dikes have burst and that the lake is pouring toward them, crushing everything in its path. They hurry and reach an abandoned, tall house on a little hill, where they decide to rest. After a short sleep, Janie wakes up and sees the lake moving closer. She and Tea Cake flee, but Motor Boat decides to stay in the house. Exhausted, the couple trudge onward, and the flooding gets so bad that they have to swim great distances. They pass bodies and horrible destruction along the way.

Trying to grab a piece of roofing for cover, Janie gets blown into rough water. She struggles but then sees a cow swimming by with a growling dog perched on its back. She grabs the cow's tail for safety, but the dog begins to attack her. Tea Cake dives to the rescue and wrestles in the water with the beast, who bites him on the cheek before he stabs it to death. The next day, Janie and Tea Cake reach Palm Beach, a scene of chaotic destruction. They find a place to rest and Janie thanks Tea Cake for saving her life.

ANALYSIS: CHAPTERS 17–18

Chapter 17 provides another glimpse of life in the muck, complicating our understanding of Janie and Tea Cake's relationship just before the climactic arrival of the hurricane in Chapter 18. Tea Cake's beating of Janie early in Chapter 17 is one of the most confusing incidents in the novel. Modern readers may be surprised that the beating has such little effect on Janie. It is tempting to attribute the briefness of Hurston's treatment of the incident to the more tolerant attitude toward domestic violence that prevailed when Hurston wrote *Their Eyes Were Watching God*. Janie's passive acceptance of the beating, however, relates to the development of her character. At this point in the story, the idea of silence becomes quite significant. Since Jody's death, Janie has struggled to find her voice. Now that she has found it, she is learning to control it. With Jody, Janie's silence is a sign of his domination and her weakness; now, silence is becoming an important part of Janie's strength. She chooses when and when not to speak. In this situation, it is implied that she is willing to sacrifice her body to satisfy Tea Cake's need for control. Her silence reflects her strength. She puts up with a beating, just once, because she feels that she is strong enough to withstand it and because its negative effects are outweighed by her love for Tea Cake and the good things that he does for her.

In many ways, Chapter 18 is the book's climax. The battle with the hurricane is the source of the book's title and illuminates the central conflict of the novel: Janie's quasi-religious quest to find her place in the world amid confusing, unpredictable, and often threatening forces. Throughout the novel, characters have operated under the delusion that they can control their environment and secure a place for themselves in the world. Jody, in particular, demonstrates the folly of this mindset in his attempts to play God. Tea Cake exhibits this folly as well. His ease in the natural environment—his mastery of the muck, his almost supernatural skill at gambling—has made him too proud; he feels that the storm is not a threat.

But, of course, the storm humbles all. It is a force of pure destruction and chaos; furthermore, it is a force without a conscience or a consciousness. It is random and unfair, a cruel and devastating facet of a confusing universe. Throughout the novel, similar forces antagonize Janie: the doctrines to which Nanny, Logan, and Jody adhere; Mrs. Turner's racism; the sexism of Eatonville's men; and the gossip of the porch culture. Like the hurricane, these forces cause Janie pain but lack malicious intent. Janie can never defeat them, only bear them and perhaps survive them.

The episode in which Tea Cake, Janie, and Motor Boat wait out the storm is the most direct example of this conflict. Here we see the opposition between individual and environment described in the starkest terms: humans against God, Janie and her friends against nature. The conflict is framed in terms of community. Janie and Tea Cake are joined by Motor Boat in their house, and all of the people in the muck share in the same horrible communion, united together against a terrifying environment. Community and intimacy—people bonded together by circumstance—are humanity's refuge against threatening forces. Tea Cake and Janie's relationship represents the most intimate type of communal bond and once again, reciprocity is central to their relationship; each helps the other survive. Their bond represents the ultimate answer to Janie's spiritual quest. Tea Cake has helped her find her voice, and this voice has enabled her to develop a love based on reciprocity and mutual respect. This union allows her to face the storm boldly and survive the storm and subsequent conflicts.

Chapter 19

Summary

After the hurricane, death is all around Palm Beach. Two white men with rifles force Tea Cake to bury corpses. Disgusted with the work and fearful of the racism around the town (the white corpses get coffins, but the black corpses are simply dumped in a ditch and covered with quicklime), Tea Cake and Janie decide to leave surreptitiously and return to the Everglades.

Tea Cake and Janie learn that although some of their friends have died, many have survived, including Motor Boat, who miraculously stayed alive during the storm while sleeping in the abandoned house. Tea Cake works for a while rebuilding the dike. But about four weeks after their return, he comes home from work early with a bad headache. He says that he is hungry, but when Janie makes him food, he is unable to eat. At night he wakes up in a choking fit and the next day gags when trying to drink water. Janie gets Dr. Simmons, a friendly white man who is a fixture in the muck. He chats amiably with Tea Cake and hears his story. But afterward, he pulls Janie aside and tells her that he thinks that the dog that bit Tea Cake was rabid. He adds that it is probably too late to save Tea Cake but that he will order medicine from Palm Beach just in case.

Tea Cake's health deteriorates and the rabies warp his mind, filling him with delusional, paranoid thoughts. Janie doesn't tell him about the doctor's diagnosis. When she sneaks off to see if the medicine has arrived, Tea Cake accuses her of sneaking off to see Mrs. Turner's brother, who has just returned to the Everglades. She mollifies him, telling him that she went to see the doctor, and they begin to talk lovingly. But Janie grows afraid when she feels a pistol hidden under the pillow.

That night, Tea Cake is seized by more choking attacks. In the morning, Janie says that she is going to see Dr. Simmons again. Tea Cake gets angry, and when he goes outside to the outhouse, Janie checks his pistol. She finds that it is loaded with three bullets. Instead of unloading it, she sets it so that it will run through the three empty chambers before getting to a bullet, giving her time to act in case he fires at her.

When Tea Cake returns, he becomes crazier, accusing Janie of treating him wrongly. Janie sees that he is holding the pistol. He pulls the trigger once, and it clicks on the empty chamber. Janie grabs the rifle and hopes to scare him off. But he pulls the trigger twice more, and as he is about to fire again, Janie has no choice but to shoot him.

Janie is put on trial that same day. In the courtroom, all of the black people of the muck have come to watch, and Janie can feel that they, her former friends, have all turned against her; they even offer to testify against her. Dr. Simmons takes the stand in defense of Janie, but Janie gives the most powerful testimony of all, telling the court about their story and her love for Tea Cake. The all-white, all-male jury finds her innocent. The white women watching the proceedings crowd around her in solidarity while her former friends shuffle out, defeated. After the trial, Janie gives Tea Cake a royal burial.

Analysis

Chapter 19 constitutes the final leg of Janie's spiritual journey, and she suffers a great deal. In Chapter 16, the narrator notes that "[r]eal gods require blood," and Janie's trials here represent her final sacrifices on the path toward liberation and enlightenment. The first trial comes with Tea Cake's being conscripted into the racist burial crew. In contrast with Hurston's treatment of Mrs. Turner, this episode presents racism in more conventional terms: whites exerting their will on blacks. But again, the racism is presented more as an environmental force or cultural construct than an essential quality of any particular person. The white men remain nameless, and the racism seems more a product of the environment and the circumstances than anything else; Tea Cake and Janie are able to escape it by leaving the area.

The second tribulation that Janie must face is Tea Cake's disease and deterioration. Once again, Janie and Tea Cake are confronted not by a particular person but by an impersonal force: a disease that he contracts as a result of events that occur during the hurricane. The diseased Tea Cake, who flies into jealous rages, is the polar opposite of the man he once was, secure in the midst of the natural world and generally confident in his possession of Janie. In other words, this capricious force destroys Tea Cake's very essence. The moment of Tea Cake's death, though horrible for Janie to endure, reflects how much she has grown as a person and how secure she has become. Although Tea Cake means everything to her, she is able to kill him to save herself. Her relationship with him has brought her along the path of enlightenment, and now that she has achieved the horizon, she is strong enough to live on her own.

The courtroom scene is Janie's final trial. Here, she faces ostracism from the same community that nurtured her development and supported her during the hurricane, a penalty worse than any the court could impose: "It was not death she feared. It was misunderstanding." She does not need the superficial acceptance in the gossip culture of the porch—she has already dismissed that world—but she needs the community to recognize the strength of her bond with Tea Cake as well as her own fortitude.

At this point, Hurston utilizes an unusual narrative device that has been the source of much debate about the novel. For most of the second half of the story, Janie speaks without interruption. She has found her voice, and language has become her means of exploring herself, asserting herself, and enjoying human interaction. But at the trial, Hurston renders her silent. While speech has been rendered in bold, direct quotations throughout much of the novel, the narrator here summarizes Janie's statements indirectly. Janie herself does not speak to the reader. The passage reads, "She talked. . . . She just sat there and told and when she was through she hushed." Some critics have argued that this shift reflects that Janie's quest has gone unfulfilled, that she has not found her voice or the horizon. But other critics, notably Alice Walker, have argued, as Mary Ellen Washington recounts in the foreword to most modern editions of the book, that Janie's silence reflects her mastery of her own voice. This perspective is in keeping with the interpretation of Janie's passive acceptance of Tea Cake's beating her in Chapter 17 as a sign of her strength.

In any event, Janie survives the trial, but, in a final, complex commentary on race, Janie is welcomed by the white women but shunned by the black community. Again, this reversal seems to reflect Hurston's anthropological views on race: racism is a cultural construct and as such, black people are as susceptible (or potentially resistant) to its doctrines as anyone else. This final scene reinforces the broad view of humanity that informs the entire book: Janie's quest is ultimately not specifically a black person's quest or a woman's quest (although her race and gender are certainly significant) but a fundamentally human one.

CHAPTER 20

SUMMARY

After Tea Cake's funeral, the men of the muck realize how poorly they treated Janie; to appease their feelings of guilt, they beat Mrs.

Turner's brother and run him out of town again. Since the Everglades mean nothing to Janie without Tea Cake, she returns to Eatonville, taking only a package of seeds that she plans to plant in remembrance of Tea Cake.

Her story finished, Janie tells Pheoby that she is content to live in Eatonville again, having already lived her dream; she has been to the "horizon and back." She knows that the town will gossip behind her back, but she doesn't care. She says that they don't know what love really is and that they have not truly lived for themselves.

That night, in bed, Janie thinks about the horrible day that she killed Tea Cake, and her whole world becomes sad. She realizes, however, that Tea Cake gave her so much and that he will always be with her. He showed her the horizon, and now she feels at peace.

ANALYSIS

The final chapter shows Janie at full strength and utmost self-assurance. She is able to reject the community that has treated her poorly and, of her own volition, return to Eatonville. The story comes full circle as Janie's long narration catches up to the moment of her current conversation with Pheoby. This return to the opening of the novel mirrors Janie's return home. The conversation, full of self-possession and sage advice, gives the impression that Janie has become a guru of sorts—indeed, Pheoby, having heard all about Janie's fulfilling adventures, declares that she is no longer satisfied with her life. Janie has, as she claims, achieved the horizon and found her enlightenment.

That a bout of melancholy settles over Janie's room is not a sign that she has failed to reach her horizon. Rather, it allows her to demonstrate the strength that she gained along her journey. As she reflects on her experiences, "[t]he day of the gun, and the bloody body, and the courthouse . . . commence[s] to sing a sobbing sigh," once again, impersonal forces harass Janie. But the memory of Tea Cake vanquishes the sadness and fills Janie with an understanding of all that she has gained and become.

Janie has already realized that suffering and sacrifice are necessary steps on the path toward self-discovery. In *The Natural* (1952), Bernard Malamud writes: "We have two lives . . . the life we learn with and the life we live with after that. Suffering is what brings us toward happiness." This maxim is certainly applicable to Janie's situation. She has grown, struggled, and suffered; having found her voice, she is now able to begin anew. Although the body of her lover is gone, his legacy remains with her, in the person that she has become. She has achieved the unity with nature that she sought so long ago under the pear tree. Although the forces of the world may be unknowable and at times painful, she is at peace with them. Her act of "pull[ing] in her horizon" around herself reflects the harmony that she has finally established with the world around her. She has found true love, which has enabled her to find her voice.

This final image of Janie "pull[ing] in her horizon" contrasts with the opening image of men's "[s]hips at a distance." These metaphorical ships suggest that regardless of their ultimate success or failure, men dream of great accomplishments, of working on and changing their external worlds. Even if the ship comes in, it still originates as something external. Janie's pulling in her horizon shifts the field of action to the interior. Her quest requires experience of the world, of other people and places, but it is ultimately directed inward.

IMPORTANT QUOTATIONS EXPLAINED

1. Ships at a distance have every man's wish on board. For some they come in with the tide. For others they sail forever on the horizon, never out of sight, never landing until the Watcher turns his eyes away in resignation, his dreams mocked to death by Time. That is the life of men. Now, women forget all those things they don't want to remember, and remember everything they don't want to forget. The dream is the truth. Then they act and do things accordingly.

This passage, which opens Their Eyes Were Watching God, establishes the novel's unusual perspective on gender difference. Because it is the story of a woman and because it was the first major novel published by a black woman, Their Eyes Were Watching God is often classified as a feminist novel. But feminism is often associated with the idea that men and women are absolutely equal; here, the narrator immediately establishes a fundamental difference between men and women. The idea that men and women need certain things from each other recurs many times throughout the novel, as Janie searches for the man who can complement her and give her those things that she doesn't have, and Logan, Jody, and Tea Cake attempt to fill their respective needs in their respective relationships with Janie. Finally, the passage foreshadows the novel's thematic concerns: the statement about women is proud and defiant, saying that while men never really reach for their dreams, women can control their wills and chase their dreams. As the novel unfolds, Janie acts according to this notion, battling and struggling in the direction of her dreams.

2.   [Janie] was stretched on her back beneath the pear tree
      soaking in the alto chant of the visiting bees, the gold of the
      sun and the panting breath of the breeze when the inaudible
      voice of it all came to her. She saw a dust-bearing bee sink
      into the sanctum of a bloom; the thousand sister-calyxes
      arch to meet the love embrace and the ecstatic shiver of the
      tree from root to tiniest branch creaming in every blossom
      and frothing with delight. So this was a marriage! She
      had been summoned to behold a revelation. Then Janie felt
      a pain remorseless sweet that left her limp and languid.

This passage from Chapter 2 marks the beginning of Janie's spiritual and sexual awakening. She is a young girl under the care of her grandmother, and this incident propels her upon her quest to reach her horizon. The embrace between the bee and the flowers imprints itself upon Janie as an idealized vision of love—a moment of mutual, reciprocal fulfillment. The flowers arch to meet the arriving bee, and the consequent union of the two provides each partner something desired. Janie searches for such a give-and-take love over the course of the entire novel.

The passage also relates to an even deeper desire, which is the ultimate goal of the love that Janie seeks: a sense of enlightenment, of oneness with the world around her. The language of this passage is evocative of the erotic, naturalistic romanticism of Walt Whitman. Like Whitman's poetry, Hurston's prose here finds divinity and spirituality in the fertile lushness of the natural world ("the ecstatic shiver of the tree . . . frothing with delight"). Janie sees nature as she wants it to be: a world full of beauty and fulfillment. She chases after this ideal because she wants to experience a harmonization with the beautiful and wild forces that she witnesses under the pear tree. Later events—particularly the hurricane of Chapter 18—introduce a very different vision of nature, but the pear tree continues to serve as her vision of ideal love, of a perfect union with another person.

3. "Listen, Sam, if it was nature, nobody wouldn't have tuh look out for babies touchin' stoves, would they? 'Cause dey just naturally wouldn't touch it. But dey sho will. So it's caution." "Naw it ain't, it's nature, cause nature makes caution. It's de strongest thing dat God ever made, now. Fact is it's de onliest thing God every made. He made nature and nature made everything else."

This interchange, which occurs in Chapter 6, is an excerpt from a lively debate between Lige Moss and Sam Watson on the porch of Jody's store. In addition to being an excellent example of Hurston's use of dialect and idiomatic English, this dialogue speaks to Janie's developing understanding of herself in relation to the world. Here, Sam and Lige argue about the relationship between mankind and God and between themselves and the world around them. In modern terms, it is a discussion of nature versus nurture. Lige argues that humans are taught everything that they know; such a perspective implies a fundamental antagonism between humanity and the natural world. In Lige's terms, there are hot stoves everywhere, and humans must learn and be vigilant to survive. Sam, on the other hand, argues that humans are naturally cautious; such a perspective implies a fundamental harmony between humanity and the natural world. According to Sam, humans, as creatures made by God, are inherently part of nature. Over the course of the novel, Janie progresses through the obstacles that the world presents her until she finally, harmoniously, reaches the horizon that she has long sought.

QUOTATIONS

4. It was inevitable that she should accept any inconsistency and cruelty from her deity as all good worshippers do from theirs. All gods who receive homage are cruel. All gods dispense suffering without reason. Otherwise they would not be worshipped. Through indiscriminate suffering men know fear and fear is the most divine emotion. It is the stones for altars and the beginning of wisdom. Half gods are worshipped in wine and flowers. Real gods require blood.

In this passage from Chapter 16, Hurston carves out an exception to the gender dichotomy that she presents in the opening sentences of the novel. Mrs. Turner's worship of qualities that she will never possess groups her with the men whose ships "sail forever on the horizon." What is most strange about the passage, though, is the implicit comparison between Mrs. Turner and Janie. The "indiscriminate suffering" and "real blood" that may lead to wisdom could equally well belong to Janie. Janie's trip to the horizon requires her to suffer at the hands of two husbands, shoot her third, and brave a ferocious hurricane. Yet for Janie, suffering is not an end in itself. She endures it so that she may experience the fullness of life and the good that comes with the bad. Mrs. Turner, however, worships her false gods because they give her a sense of superiority over her peers and because, something of a masochist, she enjoys the pain that these gods dole out. When she is mocked for her views by others, she feels like a victim and a martyr, a feeling she finds pleasurable. The narrator's stylized description, in the paragraph just below the above quote, of her wish for "an army, terrible with banners *and swords*," illustrates the fantastic vengefulness and inflated sense of self-importance that Mrs. Turner's ostracism gives her. It is this pleasure in pain that motivates her to worship "gods who dispense suffering without reason."

5. The wind came back with triple fury, and put out the light
    for the last time. They sat in company with the others in
    other shanties, their eyes straining against crude walls and
    their souls asking if He meant
    to measure their puny might against His. They seemed to be
    staring at the dark, but their eyes were watching God.

This quotation from Chapter 18 neatly summarizes the central conflict of the novel, as Janie, Tea Cake, and Motor Boat seek refuge
from the raging hurricane outside. The struggle at the heart of the
novel is set forth in the starkest terms: humans against God, Janie
and the others against nature. It is significant that Motor Boat joins
Janie and Tea Cake in their house and that the narrator notes that
everybody is united in the same struggle. We see here that the bonds
of human interaction and intimacy provide refuge against the forces
of nature. Tea Cake and Janie share an intimacy that allows them to
struggle and survive these forces. The sense of self that Janie gains
from the love that she shares with Tea Cake enables her subse-
quently to endure another hostile force—the mean-spirited scorn of
the black women of Eatonville—and maintain her inner peace.

KEY FACTS

KEY FACTS

FULL TITLE
Their Eyes Were Watching God

AUTHOR
Zora Neale Hurston

TYPE OF WORK
Novel

GENRE
Bildungsroman (coming-of-age novel), American Southern spiritual journey

LANGUAGE
English

TIME AND PLACE WRITTEN
Written in seven weeks during 1937 while Hurston was in Haiti; published in New York

DATE OF FIRST PUBLICATION
September 1937

PUBLISHER
J.B. Lippincott, Inc.

NARRATOR
The narrator is anonymous, though it is easy to detect a distinctly Southern sensibility in the narrator's voice.

POINT OF VIEW
Though the novel is narrated in the third person, by a narrator who reveals the characters' thoughts and motives, most of the story is framed as Janie telling a story to Pheoby. The result is a narrator who is not exactly Janie but who is abstracted from her. Janie's character resonates in the folksy language and metaphors that the narrator sometimes uses. Also, much of the text relishes in the immediacy of dialogue.

TONE
The narrator's attitude toward Janie, which Hurston appears to share, is entirely sympathetic and affirming.

TENSE
  Past

SETTING (TIME)
  The early twentieth century, presumably the 1920s or 1930s

SETTING (PLACE)
  Rural Florida

PROTAGONIST
  Janie

MAJOR CONFLICT
  During her quest for spiritual fulfillment, Janie clashes with the values that others impose upon her.

RISING ACTION
  Janie's jettisoning of the materialistic desires of Nanny, Logan, and Jody; her attempt to balance self-assertion with her love for Tea Cake; the hurricane—this progression pushes her toward the eventual conflict between her environment (including the people around her) and her need to understand herself.

CLIMAX
  The confrontation between Janie and the insane Tea Cake in Chapter 19 marks the moment at which Janie asserts herself in the face of the most difficult obstacle.

FALLING ACTION
  Janie's decision to shoot Tea Cake demonstrates that she has the strength to save herself even though it means killing the man she loves; the white women's support of Janie points toward the importance of individuality as a means of breaking down stereotypes.

THEMES
  Language as a mechanism of control; power and conquest as a means to fulfillment; love and relationships versus independence; spiritual fulfillment; materialism

MOTIFS
  Community, race and racism, the folklore quality of religion

SYMBOLS
  Janie's hair, the pear tree, the horizon, the hurricane

FORESHADOWING

In Chapter 1, we learn that Janie has been away from her town
for a long time and that she ran off with a younger man named
Tea Cake; Janie then tells Pheoby that Tea Cake is "gone."
The entire beginning, then, foreshadows the culmination of
Janie's journey.

STUDY QUESTIONS & ESSAY TOPICS

STUDY QUESTIONS

1. *Discuss the role of conversation in* THEIR EYES WERE WATCHING GOD. *In particular, discuss the effect of Hurston's narrative technique of alternating between highly figurative narration and colloquial dialogue.*

One of the most interesting aspects of *Their Eyes Were Watching God* is Hurston's interweaving of Standard Written English on the part of the narrator and early twentieth-century Southern black vernacular speech on the part of her characters. The extended passages of dialogue celebrate the language of Southern blacks, presenting a type of authentic voice not often seen in literature. In addition to asserting the existence and richness of Southern black culture, Hurston's use of dialogue articulates thematic concerns of the novel. For example, Hurston uses language to express the difference between Janie's relationship with Tea Cake and her relationship with Jody. When Janie meets Jody, we do not hear her speak to him; instead, the narrator *tells* us, in Standard Written English, that they talk, giving us few of their actual words. Janie's interactions with Tea Cake, on the other hand, are full of long passages of vernacular dialogue, a reflection of their genuine connection and mutual respect for each other. Throughout the novel, Janie struggles to find her own voice; Hurston demonstrates the importance of this quest with her use of dialogue as a narrative device.

2. *Explain the significance of the book's title. How does it relate to Janie's quest and the rest of the book?*

One important feature of the title *Their Eyes Were Watching God* is that the first word is plural, which anticipates the issues of community and partnership with which the novel concerns itself. As much as the story is about one woman's quest, it is also the story of how that quest is achieved both through and against community and partnership. The title is drawn from a moment in which three people act together against a threatening force—the hurricane, in Chapter 18—but soon afterward, Janie and Tea Cake split up with Motor Boat, and Janie is later forced to shoot Tea Cake. The "Their" in the title seems a fragile construct.

The novel's concept of God, the other pregnant word in the title, is most clearly articulated when the narrator describes Mrs. Turner's obsession with white features and social norms. Gods, the reader is told, require suffering, and this suffering is the beginning of wisdom. The lesson that the hurricane seems to offer is that God is all-powerful and will damn the proud like Tea Cake, who believes that his mastery of the muck will allow him to weather the hurricane. The novel's overall tenor, however, is hardly one of awed submission and humility. Janie is focused on understanding herself, not God, and exhibits a high degree of autonomy in achieving this goal. Though external forces and circumstances may demand sacrifice and suffering, Janie herself still determines the course of her life.

3. *Why is Janie initially attracted to Jody? Why does this attraction fade?*

Jody comes along at a transitional period in Janie's life. She is still partially under the spell of her grandmother's philosophy, prizing material wealth and status, but at the same time has begun to search for something greater. She is unsure what that something is but knows that it involves something more than what she has with Logan Killicks. When Jody arrives, full of bluster and ambition, he reconciles Janie's upbringing with her desire for adventure. His talk of power and conquest soothes Janie's disenchantment while his ambitious social climbing satisfies the values that Nanny has imparted to her.

Janie's interest in Jody ultimately wanes because she discovers that the role he wants her to fit offers her no fulfillment. She learns that there are two reasons that Jody will never help her achieve her dreams. First, Jody's quest is for material and social gain. He wants wealth, power, and status. No accumulation of such things, however, will help Janie in her spiritual quest. Second, Jody defines himself through his control of others, especially through his silencing of Janie. Their marriage fails because Janie refuses to tolerate Jody's inflated sense of himself any longer. His egotism, based on power over others, demands that he control and dominate Janie, which prevents her from exploring and expressing herself.

REVIEW & RESOURCES

SUGGESTED ESSAY TOPICS

1. *In 1937, Richard Wright reviewed* THEIR EYES WERE WATCHING GOD *and wrote: "The sensory sweep of her novel carries no theme, no message, no thought. In the main, her novel is not addressed to the Negro, but to a white audience whose chauvinistic tastes she knows how to satisfy." In particular, Wright objected to the novel's discussion of race and use of black dialect. Why might Wright have objected to* THEIR EYES WERE WATCHING GOD? *Do you agree or disagree with Wright's interpretation of the novel?*

2. *Discuss the idea of the horizon in the* THEIR EYES WERE WATCHING GOD. *What does it symbolize for Janie?*

3. *Compare and contrast Janie's three marriages. What initially pulls her to each of the three men? How do they differ from one another? What does she learn from each experience?*

4. *In her marriage to Jody, Janie is dominated by his power. At several points, however, it is obvious that he feels threatened by her. Why does Jody need to be in control of everyone around him? How does Janie threaten Jody and his sense of control?*

5. THEIR EYES WERE WATCHING GOD *is concerned with issues of speech and how speech is both a mechanism of control and a vehicle of liberation. Yet Janie remains silent during key moments in her life. Discuss the role of silence in the book and how that role changes throughout the novel.*

REVIEW & RESOURCES

QUIZ

1. When the novel begins, Janie is

   A. A young girl living with her grandmother
   B. About to marry Logan Killicks
   C. Arriving in Eatonville for the first time with her new husband
   D. A middle-aged woman returning to Eatonville alone

2. To whom does Janie tell the story of her life?

   A. The townspeople on the porch
   B. Her friend Pheoby Watson
   C. Her new husband, Tea Cake
   D. Nobody

3. Janie's grandfather was

   A. A slave-owner who raped Nanny
   B. Jody Starks's father's best friend
   C. A wealthy black landowner
   D. Captain Eaton

4. Whom does Janie marry first?

   A. Jody Starks
   B. Logan Killicks
   C. Vergible Woods
   D. Stubby Clapp

5. Why does Janie leave her first husband?

   A. To go to the Everglades with Tea Cake
   B. To marry Jody Starks and go to Eatonville
   C. To care for her ailing grandmother
   D. To sail a ship out to sea

REVIEW & RESOURCES

6. After Jody and Janie's arrival, what becomes the center of Eatonville's social life?

   A. Jody and Janie's house
   B. Sam Watson's porch
   C. The jook joint
   D. Jody's store

7. What does Jody, out of jealousy, force Janie to do?

   A. Stay at home every weekend
   B. Never talk to another man
   C. Tie her hair up in head-rags
   D. Wear a veil over her face

8. About what do the other men tease Matt Bonner?

   A. His sexual prowess
   B. His mule
   C. His chickens
   D. His big butt

9. For what implied reason does Jody buy Matt's mule?

   A. To make Janie happy
   B. To scam Matt Bonner
   C. To impress the town
   D. To get a cheap meal

10. What reason does Jody give for excluding Janie from the mule's funeral?

   A. Because such a "common" gathering is unfit for the mayor's wife
   B. Because he is afraid that she is too weak to handle the sight of the dead mule
   C. Because she had said that she didn't want to go
   D. Because she needs to save her energy for working in the store

11. What do Sam and Lige argue over after the mule's funeral?

    A. The mule's name

    B. Whether or not Matt Bonner treated it right

    C. Whether nature or caution keeps men away from hot stoves

    D. Whether lemon-lime soda is sweet or sour

12. On the store porch, why does Janie break her silence?

    A. To insult Jody's appearance

    B. To tell the men on the porch that they don't know as much about woman as they think they do

    C. To express her love for Jody

    D. To tell Pheoby Watson and the other women how poorly Jody treats her

13. Why, primarily, does Jody insult Janie's appearance?

    A. To appease his jealousy by making other men think that Janie is unattractive

    B. To deflect attention from his own deteriorating appearance

    C. To punish Janie for her infidelity

    D. To make Janie laugh

14. What does Jody do after Janie insults him in front of the other men?

    A. He hits Janie as hard as he can

    B. He laughs in a futile attempt to diffuse the tension

    C. He realizes how terribly he has behaved and apologizes

    D. He violently throws her out of town

15. What do the townspeople think as Jody grows sicker?

    A. That Janie is cheating on him

    B. That his years of fast living have finally caught up to him

    C. That God is punishing him for his sins

    D. That Janie is poisoning him

16. What does Janie do while visiting Jody on his deathbed?

    A.   She mercilessly berates him
    B.   She forgives him for the way that he treated her
    C.   She remains silent
    D.   She sleeps with him one last time

17. Why does Janie reject so many suitors after Jody's death?

    A.   Because she is too upset about Jody's death
    B.   Because they only want her money
    C.   Because she loves her newfound independence
    D.   Because she is secretly dating Tea Cake

18. What is Tea Cake's given name?

    A.   Robert Zimmerman
    B.   Amos Hicks
    C.   Vergible Woods
    D.   Stubby Clapp

19. What does Tea Cake show Janie on the evening of their first conversation?

    A.   A map of his land in the Everglades
    B.   How to shoot a gun
    C.   His secret pirate treasure
    D.   How to play checkers

20. Why is the town suspicious of Janie's relationship with Tea Cake?

    A.   Because Tea Cake has a criminal past
    B.   Because Tea Cake is too common for the mayor's widow
    C.   Because Tea Cake is really Logan Killicks in disguise
    D.   Because Tea Cake is secretly working for Dr. Evil

21. What term does the novel use to refer to the Everglades?

    A.   "The muck"
    B.   "The Goop"
    C.   "The veldt"
    D.   "Jersey City"

22. During the first week of their marriage, how many times does Tea Cake leave Janie alone for an extended period of time while she worries?

    A. Never
    B. Once
    C. Twice
    D. Four times

23. What is Mrs. Turner's opinion of black people?

    A. That they are all individuals deserving respect
    B. That they should try to be more like white people
    C. That they need to rise up in revolution against "the man"
    D. That white people should be more like them

24. What is the direct cause of Tea Cake's death?

    A. The hurricane
    B. The bite of a rabid dog
    C. An angry gambler with a knife
    D. A rifle shot by Janie

25. How do Janie's black friends act toward her during her trial?

    A. They are supportive of her but don't testify because of racist pressure
    B. They testify on her behalf despite racist pressure
    C. They turn their backs on her
    D. They sit quietly and refrain from judging her

Suggestions for Further Reading

Bloom, Harold, ed. *Major Black American Writers Through the Harlem Renaissance.* New York: Chelsea House Publishers, 1995.

———, ed. Zora Neale Hurston's Their Eyes Were Watching God. New York: Chelsea House Publishers, 1987.

Cooper, Jan. "Zora Neale Hurston Was Always a Southerner Too." In *The Female Tradition in Southern Literature,* ed. Carol S. Manning. Chicago: University of Illinois Press, 1993.

Gates, Henry Louis Jr. Afterword to *Their Eyes Were Watching God,* by Zora Neale Hurston. New York: HarperPerennial, 1998.

Gates, Henry Louis Jr. "*Their Eyes Were Watching God*: Hurston and the Speakerly Text." In *Zora Neale Hurston: Critical Perspectives Past and Present,* ed. Henry Louis Gates Jr. and K.A. Appiah. New York: Amistad Press, 1993.

Lee, Spike. *Spike Lee's Gotta Have It.* New York: Simon & Schuster, 1987.

Walker, Alice. Dedication to *I Love Myself When I am Laughing . . . and Then Again When I Am Looking Mean and Impressive: A Zora Neale Hurston Reader,* ed. Alice Walker. New York: The Feminist Press, 1979.

Washington, Mary Helen. Foreword to *Their Eyes Were Watching God,* by Zora Neal Hurston. New York: HarperPerennial, 1998.